500 CUPS

500 CUPS

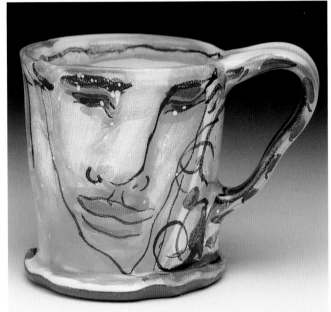

Ceramic Explorations
of Utility & Grace

LARK BOOKS

A Division of Sterling Publishing Co., Inc.
New York

Editor: **Suzanne J.E. Tourtillott**
Art Director: **Kathleen Holmes**
Cover Designer: **Barbara Zaretsky**
Assistant Editor: **Rebecca Guthrie**
Associate Art Director: **Shannon Yokeley**
Editorial Assistance: **Delores Gosnell, Rosemary Kast, Jeff Hamilton**
Editorial Intern: **Meghan McGuire, Matthew M. Paden, Amanda Wheeler**

Library of Congress Cataloging-in-Publication Data

    500 cups : explorations of utility & grace / [editor, Suzanne J.E. Tourtillott].– 1st ed.
       p. cm.
    Includes index.
    ISBN 1-57990-593-5 (pbk.)
    1. Drinking cups–History–21st century–Catalogs.   I. Title: Five hundred cups. II. Tourtillott, Suzanne J. E.
    NK4695.C8A145 2005
    738—dc22

                    2004012258

10 9 8 7 6 5 4 3 2 1

First Edition
Published by Lark Books, A Division of Sterling Publishing Co., Inc.
387 Park Avenue South, New York, N.Y. 10016

© 2004, Lark Books

Distributed in Canada by Sterling Publishing,
c/o Canadian Manda Group, 165 Dufferin Street
Toronto, Ontario, Canada M6K 3H6

Distributed in the U.K. by Guild of Master Craftsman Publications Ltd.,
Castle Place, 166 High Street, Lewes, East Sussex, England BN7 1XU
Tel: (+ 44) 1273 477374, Fax: (+ 44) 1273 478606,
Email: pubs@thegmcgroup.com, Web: www.gmcpublications.com

Distributed in Australia by Capricorn Link (Australia) Pty Ltd.,
P.O. Box 704, Windsor, NSW 2756 Australia

If you have questions or comments about this book, please contact:

Lark Books
67 Broadway
Asheville, NC 28801
(828) 253-0467

Manufactured in China

ISBN 1-57990-593-5

Cover: Elizabeth Flannery *Shibori Cup*, 2003
Title page: Ann Tubbs *Face Mug*, 2004

Contents: Suze Lindsay *Set of Tumblers*, 2004; **Joanna Stecker** *Teacup and Pillow*, 2003; **Ruchika Madan** *Blue Mug*, 2003; **Kevin L. Turner** *Solenopsis Pair*, 2003; **Mary E. Briggs** *Bird with Blueberries*, 2003; **Karin Solberg** *Cups*, 2003; **Al Tennant** *T Bowl*, 2003; **John Williams** *Map Cup*, 2004; **Stephen Grimmer** *Three Bourbon Cups on Stand*, 2003

CONTENTS

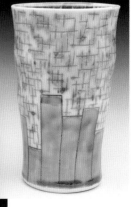

INTRODUCTION

The cup, oh, the lowly cup! What actually constitutes a cup? The dictionary describes it as a small open container, usually with a flat bottom and sometimes a handle, used for drinking. From some early, hard lessons in art school I concluded that an acceptable functional cup should be made as a form that accommodates the hand, the eye, and the lip. It should have good balance and convey a sense of design. The handle, if it has one, should resemble a fluid brush stroke that seems to be growing from the body of the cup.

The Japanese have always thought of drinking from their teabowls as drinking from nature. Kim Stafford, a well-known Oregon poet, was asked to write about the experience of drinking from a certain wood-fired cup, and she replied that it was like drinking from a tide pool. What a wonderful picture this conjures up!

For this book, Elaine and I viewed well over 2,000 images and we enjoyed looking at all the different expressions of the cup. And although we have our preferences, we tried to choose a wide assortment of styles and techniques that will give you an idea of how individual artists of today perceive this ubiquitous form, whether it be a mug, a tea bowl, or a cup perched on a stem.

A good variety of cups were submitted that ranged from strictly functional—almost commercially smooth—work, as seen in Benjamin Schulman's "Stacked Teacup Set," to highly altered forms with a distinctly functional bent, as in Heather O'Brien's "Dessert Cups on Stand." Innovative decorative techniques were employed by artists such as Lauren Gallaspy, who used pencil-like lines to make incredible drawings on "Slitten," while Annette Gates embellished a bold, footed cup form with simple abstract lines, dots of glaze, and jewels in her "Espresso Shot Cups With Rubies." In fact, this book has a large selection of work devoted to decorative technique, a range exemplified by the exuberant low-fired majolica overglaze by Farraday Newsome, as well as the restrained Japanese brushwork on high-fired porcelain by Sam Scott.

Two artists present work in the style of Old English Toby Mugs, using the human head as inspiration for the form of their cups. Andrea E. Hull sculpts tender, moody faces, as in her "Untitled Pair #1," with soft, painted surfaces applied as delicately as one would apply makeup, while Nobuhito Nishigawara uses a stark white glaze to create a very different mood. Cups by artists such as Barbara Tipton borrow from conceptual art, using the idea of a cup as an art form.

A number of clay artists make cups that are both sculptural and humorous. Among these were Jim Koudelka's "Primary Cup and Saucer," Joan Pevarnik's "Caught," and Robert "Boomer" Moore's "Come Along Cup." Such an approach tends to make the viewer see the cup in a different light—not only as a functional object, but perhaps as the means of a more overt or, at the least, lighthearted kind of artistic expression.

Wood-fired, soda-fired, and multiple shino-glazed pieces abound. Since Elaine and I were trained in the Japanese tradition, we must admit we tend to lean toward work in this area. Ten years ago most galleries owners wouldn't take a second look at work done in this style. But the public's interest has been sparked because of artists like Malcom Davis, with his carbon trap shinos, and young artists such as Matt Long, who use soda-fired shinos, along with ceramists such as Al Tennant and Tony Ferguson, who employ incredible textures and warm, rich colors on their wood-fired tea bowls. In recent years these types of cups have become much more desirable, so it's a pleasure to be able to include so many fine examples.

As we spent those many nights in a dark room looking at the slides of cups, we started thinking about how wonderfully different clay is from every other media. It is a functional material and yet can be a form of art in itself (after all, it's hard to drink from a painting!). To us, the most important part about clay has always been the tactile: to hold a cup and see it as a piece of art and at the same time use it is a wonderful thing.

This makes me think about an old friend of ours who happened to be blind. He called our studio one day, very discouraged, explaining that he had broken his favorite cup. I asked him, Don't you have several others similar to that one? He replied that he did, but that was the only one that had a certain feel, that fit his hand just right. This conversation made me reflect on how often we choose things in life by the way they look. Can great craftsmanship and quality be detected by touch alone? Does it have to be visual to be good? Certainly these are essential, but my friend's sense of the matter is one that I share: it is the tactile experience of drinking from a handmade cup that creates one's fullest appreciation for it.

Jurying for this book was a challenging task. Choosing 500 of anything good in life will always be difficult. We would like to thank and congratulate all the artists who sent work for our consideration. The good cups helped make it easy.

TOM COLEMAN

Previous page top row: Elaine Coleman
Incised Blue Celadon Leaf and Flower Cup, 2003. 4½ x 3½ in. (11.4 x 8.9 cm) Thrown, altered, and incised high-fire porcelain; reduction, cone 10
Incised Yellow Celadon Lizard and Leaf Cup, 2003. 4½ x 3¾ in. (11.4 x 9.5 cm) Thrown, altered, and incised high-fire porcelain; reduction, cone 10
Incised Green Celadon Butterfly and Leaf Cup, 2004. 4½ x 3½ in. (11.4 x 8.9 cm) Thrown, altered, and incised high-fire porcelain; reduction, cone 10. All photos by Tom Coleman

Bottom row: Tom Coleman *Thrown and Altered Cup*, 2004. 4 x 3¾ in. (10.2 x 9.5 cm) Thrown and altered porcelain; reduction, cone 10; ash glaze over colored slips
Thrown and Altered Cup with Handle, 2003. 5½ x 3½ in. (14 x 8.9 cm) Thrown and altered porcelain; reduction, cone 10; ash glaze
Thrown and Altered Cup, 2004. 4 x 3¾ in. (10.2 x 9.5 cm) Thrown and altered porcelain; reduction, cone 10; multiple carbon trap shinos. All photos by artist

JINNY WHITEHEAD

Cup, 2003

3½ x 2½ in. (8.9 x 6.4 cm)
Thrown porcelain; wood fired,
cone 12; thin shino glaze
Photo by Eye Q Studios
(Duff & Gravelsins)

DAVIE RENEAU
Tea Bowl with Assiette, 2003

4½ x 3 x 3½ in.
(11.4 x 7.6 x 8.9 cm)
Wheel-thrown and hand-built
porcelain and stoneware;
anagama fired, cone 11
Photo by Bob Payne

THIS PIECE IS ABOUT THE CONTRAST
BETWEEN THE PRECISE CUTS OF THE TEA
BOWL AND THE RIPPED, TORN EDGES OF
THE ASSIETTE, WHICH WAS MADE FROM A
CRUNCHY LOCAL STONEWARE.

WILLIAM BAKER
Tumbler, 2003

4$\frac{1}{2}$ x 3 x 3 in. (11.4 x 7.6 x 7.6 cm)
Wheel-thrown and altered stoneware;
salt and soda fired, cone 10; kaolin slip
Photo by artist

BARBARA KNUTSON
Footed Cup, 2000

4 x 5 x 3½ in. (10.2 x 12.7 x 8.9 cm)
Slab-built white stoneware; reduction
fired, cone 10; pressed spirals,
rolled dots, hollow handle
Photo by Tim Barnwell

JACOB PRATER
Tea Bowl, 2003

2½ x 3½ x 2 in.
(6.4 x 8.9 x 5 cm)
Wheel-thrown white
stoneware; wood fired,
cone 10; slip decoration
Photo by artist

AL TENNANT
T Bowl, 2003

4 x 4 in. (10.2 x 10.2 cm)
Thrown stoneware; wood
fired in anagama kiln,
cone 13; reduction cooled,
cone 07; dry shino glaze
Photo by Steve Sauer
Collection of Chuck Hindes

PIA SILLEM
Misgiven, 2003

3 x 4 in. (7.6 x 10.2 cm)
Thrown porcelain; wood
fired; shino glaze
Photo by Eye Q Studios
(Duff & Gravelsins)

MALCOLM DAVIS
Shino Tea Bowl, 2003

3¼ x 3 in. (8.3 x 7.6 cm)
Thrown porcelain; gas fired, cone
10; carbon trap shino glaze
Photo by D. James Dee

JOANNA STECKER
Leaf Teacup Set, 2003

4 x 6 x 6 in. each (10.2 x 15.2 x 15.2 cm)
Thrown and hand-built porcelain; salt
fired, cone 10
Photo by artist

KRISTEN KIEFFER | 4½ x 7 x 6 in. each (11.4 x 17.8 x 15.2 cm)
Cup and Saucer, 2003 | Thrown and stamped white stoneware; soda
fired, cone 10; slip trailed
Photo by the artist

LISA KARMAZIN
Cup and Saucer, 2001

6 x 5 x 4 in.
(15.2 x 12.7 x 10.2 cm)
Wheel-thrown and
altered porcelain; electric
oxidation, cone 6
Photo by David Harrison

NENA ESCOBAR
360° Cups, 2003

5 x 3½ x 5 in. each
(12.7 x 8.9 x 12.7 cm)
Wheel-thrown porcelain;
oxidation fired, cone 9
Photo by artist

WYNNE WILBUR | 5 x 4½ x 3 in.
Warm Pear Cup, 2003 | (12.7 x 11.4 x 7.6 cm)
Wheel-thrown terra cotta; electric
fired, cone 03; majolica
Photo by artist

KAREN NEWGARD | 5 x 3½ x 3½ in. each (12.7 x 8.9 x 8.9 cm)
Cups, 2004 | Wheel-thrown porcelain; salt fired, cone 10;
terra sigillata, sgraffito
Photo by Walker Montgomery

KARIN SOLBERG | 4 x 3 x 3 in. each (10.2 x 7.6 x 7.6 cm)
Cups, 2003 | Thrown and altered porcelain; salt
fired, cone 11; inlaid slips with glaze
Photo by artist

KIMBERLY DAVY
Forbidden Fruit, 2003

$4^3/4$ x $3^1/2$ x $3^1/2$ in. (12 x 8.9 x 8.9 cm)
Thrown, carved, and altered porcelain
with sprig-mold application; oxidation
fired, cone 6; polychrome glaze
Photo by artist

I DECORATE AND RECONSTRUCT TRADITIONAL
POTTERY FORMS. IN DOING SO, I WISH TO COM-
MUNICATE MY NOTION OF THE WORLD THAT
CURRENTLY AFFECTS AND SURROUNDS ME. I
LOOK FOR TRUTH TO BLEED OUT FROM THE
INTERIOR, AN EXPRESSION THAT BECOMES EXAG-
GERATED THROUGH CARVED FEATURES AND THE
USE OF GLAZE COLOR AND SURFACE DECORATION.

KATHY ADAMS
Carved Porcelain Teacup, 2003

2½ x 2½ x 2½ in. (6.4 x 6.4 x 6.4 cm)
Wheel-thrown and carved porcelain;
wood fired, cone 11
Photo by Walker Montgomery

JOANNE TAYLOR BROWN
Lumpy Cup, 2003

5 x 6 x 4 in.
(12.7 x 15.2 x 10.2 cm)
Slab-built porcelain;
reduction fired, cone 10;
celadon glaze
Photo by Melissa Enders

TED NEAL | 7 x 5 x 5 in.
SWBT Co., 2000 | (17.8 x 12.7 x 12.7 cm)
Wheel-thrown stoneware;
soda-vapor fired, cone 10;
sandblasted; steel wire,
found objects
Photo by artist

STEPHEN HEYWOOD
Two Lidded Cups with Saucers, 2002

5 x 8 x 4 in. each (12.7 x 20.3 x 10.2 cm)
Wheel-thrown stoneware; soda fired,
cone 10; crackle slip and slip stencil
Photo by artist

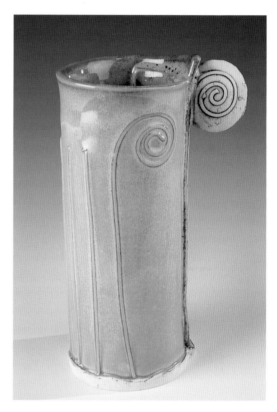

CHUCK McMAHON
Squared Tea Bowl, 2004

4 x 3 x 3 in.
(10.2 x 7.6 x 7.6 cm)
Thrown and altered
stoneware; soda fired,
cone 10
Photo by artist

SARAH DUNSTAN
Porcelain Cup, 2003

4¾ x 1⅝ in. (12 x 4 cm)
Slab-built porcelain;
electric, cone 9
Photo by Steve Tanner

LUCY FAGELLA | 5½ x 3 in. each (14 x 7.6 cm)
Three Goblet Forms, 2003 | Thrown, altered, and stamped
porcelain; electric fired, cone 6
Photo by John Polak

CAROLINE CERCONE
Yonomi Teacup, 2004

3 x 3 x 3½ in. (7.6 x 7.6 x 8.9 cm)
Thrown stoneware; gas fired in reduction, cone 10; layered shino, ash glaze, wax resist, and slip application
Photo by artist

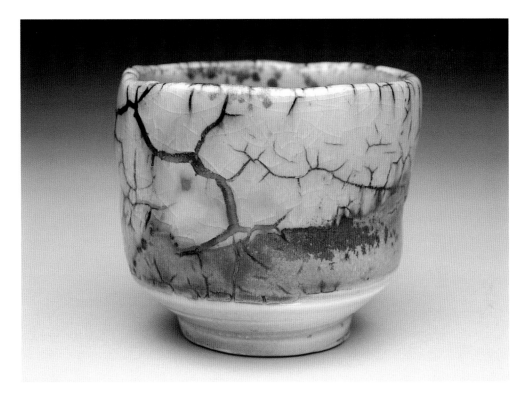

AL TENNANT | 4 x 4 in. (10.2 x 10.2 cm)
T Bowl, 2003 | Wheel-thrown porcelain; wood fired
in anagama kiln, cone 13; reduction
cooled, cone 07
Photo by Steve Sauer

JANICE MANN
Bulls-eye, 2004

4 x 4½ x 4½ in.
(10.2 x 11.4 x 11.4 cm)
Wheel-thrown, altered, and
carved porcelain; salt fired,
cone 10; underglaze and glazes
Photo by Lee Schwabe

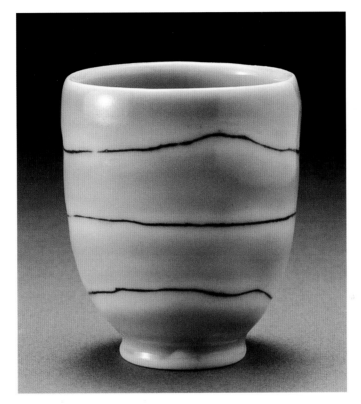

KELLY O'BRIANT
Little Cup with Lines, 2003

$2\frac{1}{2}$ x $1\frac{1}{2}$ x $1\frac{1}{2}$ in.
(6.4 x 3.8 x 3.8 cm)
Wheel-thrown porcelain;
methane gas fired, cone $10\frac{1}{2}$;
terra sigillata, celadon glaze
Photo by Tom Mills

JOHN A. VASQUEZ
*Espresso Cup and
Saucer, 2003*

2³⁄₄ x 3¹⁄₂ x 3¹⁄₂ in.
(7 x 8.9 x 8.9 cm)
Thrown stoneware; gas
fired with salt and soda,
cone 10; copper glaze,
kaolin slips, and black
underglaze
Photo by Tom Mills

MINDY ANDREWS
Forest Floor, 2004

4¹⁄₄ x 6 x 4 in.
(10.8 x 15.2 x 10.2 cm)
Wheel-thrown and carved
porcelain; gas fired with
salt, cone 10; slip decoration
Photo by artist

COLLETTE SMITH

Altered Square Cup and Saucer with Glaze Windows, 2003

Cup: 3 x 3½ x 3½ in.
(7.6 x 8.9 x 8.9 cm)
Saucer: 1½ x 6½ x 6½ in.
(3.8 x 16.5 x 16.5 cm)
Thrown white stoneware; gas fired in reduction, cone 10; ash glaze with celadon windows, colored slip; brushwork
Photo by Joe Guinta

ZANE WILCOX
Cup, 2003

$3\frac{1}{2}$ x $3\frac{1}{2}$ x $3\frac{1}{2}$ in.
(8.9 x 8.9 x 8.9 cm)
Wheel-thrown stoneware;
salt fired, cone 10
Photos by Grant Kernan

DAVEN HEE
Empty Calories, 2003

$3^{1}/_{2}$ x $4^{1}/_{2}$ x $4^{1}/_{2}$ in.
(8.9 x 11.4 x 11.4 cm)
Wheel-thrown and cut
stoneware; wood fired in
anagama kiln, cone 11
Photos by Brad Goda

CAROL ANN WEDEMEYER
Tooth Cup, 2001

5¹⁄₂ x 6 x 5 in.
(14 x 15.2 x 12.7 cm)
Coil-built, slab-built,
and pinched B-Mix;
cone 5; sanded
Photo by Wilfred J. Jones

THIS SMOOTH, ORGANIC FORM
HAS A TACTILE DRAW, WITH
LINES THAT LEAD YOUR EYE TO
THE INSIDE OF THE CUP. CARE
WAS TAKEN TO MAKE THE INTE-
RIOR SMOOTH AND LOVELY TOO.

ERIC REMPE
*Memories of You:
A Toasting Glass*, 2003

5 x 5 x 5 in.
(12.7 x 12.7 x 12.7 cm)
Wheel-thrown and altered
stoneware and porcelain; gas
fired in reduction, cone 10;
rubber-coated stoneware base
Photo by Michael Campos
Collection of Justin Johnson

MICHELLE TINNER
Cup and Saucer, 2003

$4\frac{1}{2}$ x $5\frac{1}{2}$ x $4\frac{1}{2}$ in.
(11.4 x 14 x 11.4 cm)
Slip-cast porcelain; electric fired,
cone 6
Photo by artist

TODD REDMOND | 7 x 5 x 3 in.
Striped Mug, 2003 | (17.8 x 12.7 x 7.6 cm)
Hand-built porcelain;
reduction, cone 10
Photo by Glenn Asakawa

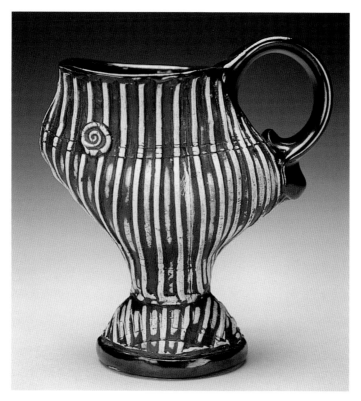

RACHEL BLEIL
Black and White Mug, 2002

$5\frac{1}{2}$ x $5\frac{1}{2}$ x 3 in.
(14 x 14 x 7.6 cm)
Slab-built white earthenware;
electric fired, cone 06; black
slip and glaze
Photo by artist

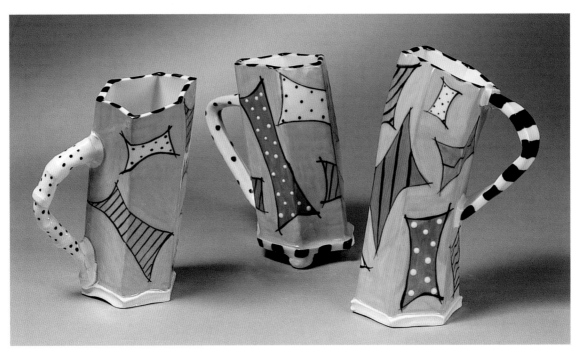

KIMBERLY RORICK
Extruded Cups, 2000

6¹/₂ x 4 in. each (16.5 x 10.2 cm)
Extruded porcelain; electric fired,
cone 5; underglaze and glaze
Photo by John Escosa

FARRADAY NEWSOME

Light Blue Cup and Saucer with Dogwoods and Oranges, 2002

5 x 10 x 10 in.
(12.7 x 25.4 x 25.4 cm)
Thrown terra cotta; electric fired, cone 5; majolica
Photo by artist

SHARON DENNARD

Pepper Goblet, 1992

7½ x 3 x 3 in. each
(19 x 7.6 x 7.6 cm)
Cast and altered earthenware; electric fired, cone 06; glaze
Photo by Bill Dennard

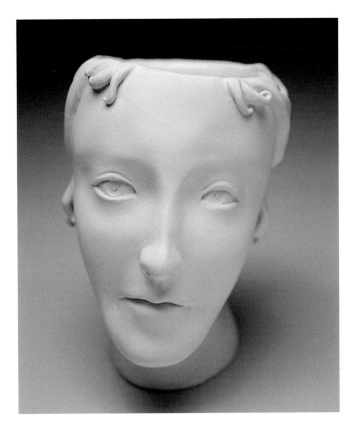

NOBUHITO NISHIGAWARA
Cup, 2003

7 x 5 x 5 in.
(17.8 x 12.7 x 12.7 cm)
Hand-built porcelain; electric
fired, cone 6; polished
Photo by artist

ANDREA E. HULL
Untitled Pair #1, 2003

I MADE THIS SET OF CUPS TO ILLUSTRATE A
DIALOGUE TWO PEOPLE MIGHT HAVE. I WAS
MOVING SOME THINGS AROUND IN MY STUDIO
ONE DAY AND SET THE CUPS IN A WAY DIFFER-
ENT THAN I HAD INITIALLY INTENDED, MAKING
A COMPLETELY DIFFERENT SITUATION. THIS
WAS EXCITING AND I NOW TRY TO BUILD THAT
AMBIGUITY INTO MY WORK.

5½ x 8 x 5 in. each (14 x 20.3 x 12.7 cm)
Pinched stoneware; electric fired,
cone 04; Mason stains, glaze
Photo by Walker Montgomery

MALCOLM DAVIS
Shino Mug, 2002

$3\frac{1}{4}$ x $3\frac{3}{4}$ x $3\frac{3}{4}$ in. (8.3 x 9.5 x 9.5 cm)
Thrown porcelain; gas fired, cone 10; carbon
trap shino glaze, wax resist brushwork
Photo by D. James Dee

GINNY CASH
Porcelain Coffee Mug, 2003

4 x $3\frac{1}{2}$ x $3\frac{1}{2}$ in. (10.2 x 8.9 x 8.9 cm)
Altered porcelain; reduction fired, cone
10; sprayed shino glaze
Photo by Jerry Dillahunt

SKEFFINGTON THOMAS | 5 x 4 x 4 in.
Mug, 1999 | (12.7 x 10.2 x 10.2 cm)
Wheel-thrown porcelain;
reduction fired, cone 10
Photo by John Carlano

SCOTT D. CORNISH | 4 x 4½ x 4 in.
Wood-Fired Mug, 2004 | (10.2 x 11.4 x 10.2 cm)
Wheel-thrown porcelain; wood
fired, cone 12; wax resist,
shino glaze, and slips
Photo by artist

JOHN GOODHEART | 8 x 4 in. (20.3 x 10.2 cm)
The Cup of Seeds, 2001 | Thrown earthenware;
electric fired, cone 05;
fabricated metal parts
Photo by Michael Cavanaugh
and Kevin Montague

JIM KOUDELKA
Primary Cup and Saucer, 1998

THIS WORK DISPLAYS MY INTEREST AND
INVOLVEMENT WITH THE VESSEL FORMAT, WHICH
IS LINKED WITH ARCHITECTURAL, MECHANICAL,
AND INDUSTRIAL IMAGES AND SURFACES.

8 x 10 x 5 in. (20.3 x 25.4 x 12.7 cm)
Thrown, molded, hand-built, and
assembled stoneware; salt fired, cone
10; multiple low-fire glazes, cone 06;
metal chain; sandblasted
Photo by artist

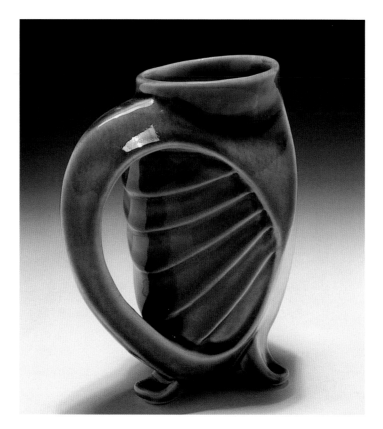

MARK BRANSTINE
Grasshopper, 2004

6 x 5¼ x 3¼ in.
(15.2 x 13.3 x 8.3 cm)
Slab-built porcelain; gas fired in
reduction, cone 10; celadon glaze
with red overspray; white liner glaze
Photo by artist

SYLVIA RAMACHANDRAN
Sighing Herb, 2003

4 x 4 x 1½ in. (10.2 x 10.2 x 3.8 cm)
Slab-built and carved whiteware;
electric fired, cone 04; multi-fired
layers of underglaze and clear glaze,
cones 04 and 06
Photo by Hawkinson Photography

MY DESIGNS COMBINE GESTURES
OBSERVED IN PLANTS AND ANIMALS. MY
GOAL IS TO UNDERSTAND THE IMPULSES
HUMANS SHARE WITH OTHER LIVING
THINGS AND WITH EACH OTHER.

JODY WEBER
Cup and Saucer, 2002

4½ x 7 x 7 in. (11.4 x 17.8 x 17.8 cm)
Wheel-thrown and stamped porcelain;
reduction fired, cone 10
Photo by artist

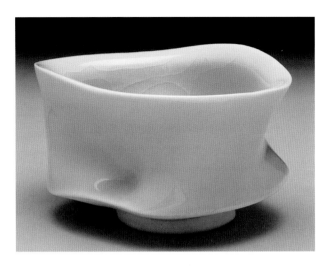

DAVID PIPER

Drinking Cup, 2003

4 x 4 x 4 in.
(10.2 x 10.2 x 10.2 cm)
Thrown porcelain; reduction
fired, cone 9; celadon glaze
Photo by Leslie Bauer

PAULINE PELLETIER

Pimento Mug, 2003

4 x 3¼ in. (10.2 x 8.3 cm)
Cast porcelain; gas fired in
reduction, cone 11; gold luster,
cone 018; green celadon glaze
Photo by C. Jalbert

KEVIN A. MYERS
Untitled Cup #2, 2004

13¾ x 7½ x 8 in.
(35 x 19 x 20.3 cm)
Thrown and altered stoneware;
cone 10; celadon and ash glazes
Photo by Anthony Cunha

KEVIN L. TURNER | $7\frac{1}{2}$ x $6\frac{1}{2}$ x $6\frac{1}{2}$ in.
Solenopsis Cup, 2003 | (19 x 16.5 x 16.5 cm)
Hand-built and slip-cast porce-
lain; reduction fired, cone 10;
glazed and sanded surface
Photo by artist

JIL FRANKE
Tea Bowl, 2002

2¼ x 2¾ x 2¾ in.
(5.7 x 7 x 7 cm)
Slab-built stoneware;
wood fired in double-
chamber Bourry box kiln,
cone 10; slip decorated
Photo by Kirk Lyttle

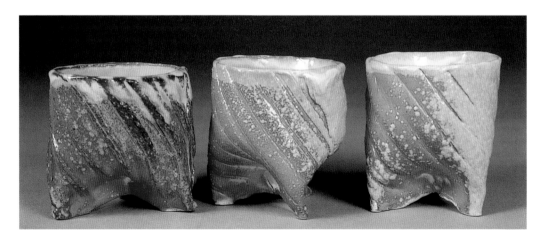

ANNE GOLDBERG,
Teacups, 2003

1½ x 2½ x 2½ in. each (3.8 x 6.4 x 6.4 cm)
Slab-built porcelain; soda fired, cone 10
Photo by artist

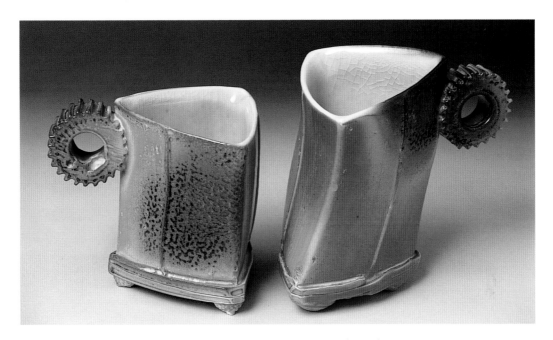

RICHARD BURKETT
Set of Two Cups for An Industrial Worker, 2003

Larger: 5 x 4½ x 3½ in.
(12.7 x 11.4 x 8.9 cm)
Extruded and hand-built porcelain;
soda fired, cone 10; carbon trapping
Photo by artist

PATRICIA G. HERZOG
Yellow Squash Cup Set, 2004

4½ x 9¼ x 5½ in. (11.4 x 23.5 x 14 cm)
Hand-built white stoneware; electric
oxidation, cone 6; layered glazes
Photo by Gary Heatherly

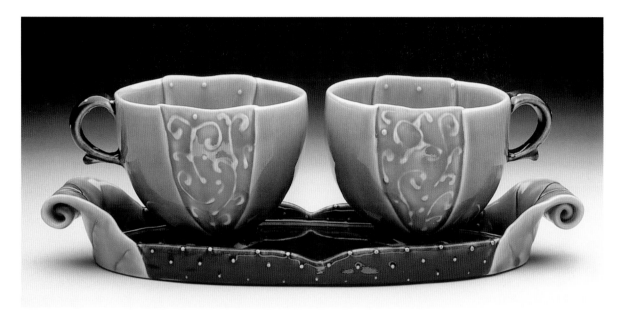

SHANNON NELSON
Tea for Two, 2000

3 x 9½ x 4 in. (7.6 x 24.1 x 10.2 cm)
Thrown, altered, hand-built, and slip-trailed
white stoneware; electric fired, cone 6
Photo by John Knaub

THADDEUS POWERS
Cup and Saucer, 2004

$4\frac{1}{4}$ x $5\frac{3}{4}$ in. (10.8 x 14.6 cm)
Thrown porcelain; salt fired in
neutral, cone 10
Photo by artist

LAURA MOORE
Mug, 2002

3 x 4 x 3½ in. (7.6 x 10.2 x 8.9 cm)
Porcelain; reduction fired, cone 10;
celadon glaze
Photo by artist

UTILITARIAN VALUES PRESENT CERTAIN DEMANDS BEYOND THE VISUAL. I FIND MYSELF CONTEMPLATING THE NEGATIVE SHAPES CONTAINED WITHIN HANDLES AND THE CHARACTER OF THE HANDLES THEMSELVES. ATTENTION TO THE NUANCES OF BALANCE, COMFORT, AND ERGONOMICS FACILITATE USE AS I ALSO STRIVE TO CONVEY GENTLE GESTURES AND CASUAL ELEGANCE THROUGH MY POTS. I HOPE TO BRING ABOUT TACTILE AND PARTICIPATORY RELATIONSHIPS BETWEEN MY WORK AND THE PEOPLE WHO USE THEM.

MICHELLE TOBIA
Three Cups, 2003

4¼ x 4 x 4 in. each (10.8 x 10.2 x 10.2 cm)
Wheel-thrown and altered porcelain;
soda fired, cone 10
Photo by artist

CONNER BURNS | 5½ x 5 x 5 in. each (14 x 12.7 x 12.7 cm)
Triple Parfait, 2003 | Wheel-thrown and altered white stoneware;
gas fired in reduction, cone 10
Photo by Al Surratt

ROBIN DUPONT
Coffee Bowl, 2003

3 x 4 x 4 in.
(7.6 x 10.2 x 10.2 cm)
Thrown stoneware; wood
fired, cone 12
Photo by Rita Taylor

DAVID ORSER
White Crag, 2002

3 x 5 x 5 in. (7.6 x 12.7 x 12.7 cm)
Wheel-thrown and hand-carved
stoneware; reduction fired, cone 10;
carbon trap glaze
Photos by artist

MARK STROM
Cup, 2003

4½ x 3 x 3 in.
(11.4 x 7.6 x 7.6 cm)
Thrown and altered
porcelain; gas fired, cone
10; incised shino glaze
with sifted ash glaze
Photo by Tom Holt

TONY FERGUSON
Winchester, 2003

3½ x 3½ x 3½ in.
(8.9 x 8.9 x 8.9 cm)
Wheel-thrown and faceted
stoneware; wood fired in
anagama kiln, cone 12;
shino and natural fly ash
Photo by artist

CUPS ARE INTRINSICALLY
SENSUAL AND NURTURING.
THEY ENGAGE THE SENSES
ON A VERY BASIC, ELEMENTAL
LEVEL. I LIKE THIS SHAPE
BECAUSE IT SEEMS TO INVITE
ONE'S HAND TO FOLD
AROUND AND CRADLE IT.

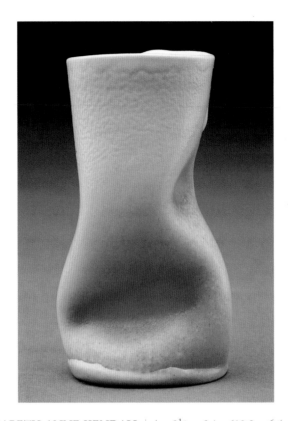

ELIZABETH ANNE KENDALL
Torso Cup, 2003

BOTH THE CHEMISTRY OF THE
PORCELAIN/SODA ASH COMBINATION AND
THE PHYSICAL UNDULATIONS OF THE
BENDING SLAB WORK TOGETHER TO
CAPTURE A BLUSH OF ORANGE. THIS SOFT
GLOW, FADING IN AND OUT AROUND THE
FORM, IS A RECORD OF THE LONG, SLOW
FLAME OF THE WOOD-BURNING KILN.

4 x 2½ x 2 in. (10.2 x 6.4 x 5 cm)
Slab-built porcelain; wood/soda
fired in reduction; Bourry kiln fired,
cone 11; white satin matte glaze;
soaked in soda ash solution
Photo by artist

GERTRUDE GRAHAM SMITH | 5 x 3½ in. (12.7 x 8.9 cm)
Tumbler, 2002 | Wheel-thrown porcelain; gas fired with
soda, cone 10
Photo by Tom Mills

JEANNINE MARCHAND
Group of Seating Cups, 2003

Smallest: 4 x 3½ in. (10.2 x 8.9 cm)
Largest: 4½ x 4 in. (11.4 x 10.2 cm)
Thrown porcelain; salt fired, cone 10
Photo by Tom Mills

CONNER McKISSACK
Coffee Mug, 2003

4 x 3½ x 3 in.
(10.2 x 8.9 x 7.6 cm)
Wheel-thrown and
altered porcelain;
soda fired, cone 10
Photo by artist

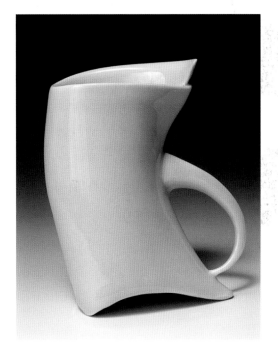

SUSAN FILLEY
Fleet Cup, 2003

5 x 3½ x 2 in.
(12.7 x 8.9 x 5 cm)
Thrown and altered
porcelain; reduction,
cone 10
Photo by artist

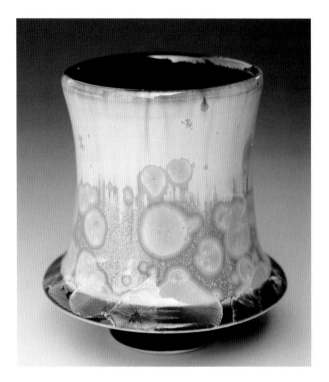

BRIAN JENSEN
Crystal Cup, 2004

6 x 4 x 4 in.
(15.2 x 10.2 x 10.2 cm)
Porcelain; cone 10;
crystalline glaze
Photo by artist

ILENE MAHLER
Crystalline Teacup, 2003

3¾ x 4 x 4½ in.
(9.5 x 10.2 x 11.4 cm)
Thrown porcelain; oxidation
fired, cone 10
Photo by R.J. Phil

AARON S. PADILLA
Cup in Boat, 2004

I SAGGAR FIRE MY PIECES SEVERAL
TIMES TO BUILD UP COLOR AND
TEXTURE ON THE SURFACE.

5½ x 5 x 2 ½ in.
(14 x 12.7 x 6.4 cm)
Hand-built stoneware; gas
fired, cone 5; saggar-fired
terra sigillata
Photo by artist

LUKE L. HELLING-
CHRISTY
Taste of Earth, 2004

13 x 9 x 5 in.
(33 x 22.9 x 12.7 cm)
Wheel-thrown, hand-built,
and slip-cast porcelain with
stoneware base; electric
fired, cone 6; additional
firings, cone 04
Photo by David Calicchio

SHANE M. KEENA
Calyx, 2001

5½ x 5 x 2½ in.
(14 x 12.7 x 6.4 cm)
Hand-built stoneware;
gas fired, cone 5; saggar-
fired terra sigillata
Photo by artist

ANDERSON MORRIS BAILEY | 7 x 8 x 4 in. (17.8 x 20.3 x 10.2 cm)
Shotcup Set, 2003 | Thrown and hand-built porcelain;
wood fired, cone 10; wax resist
with flashing slip
Photo by John Lucas

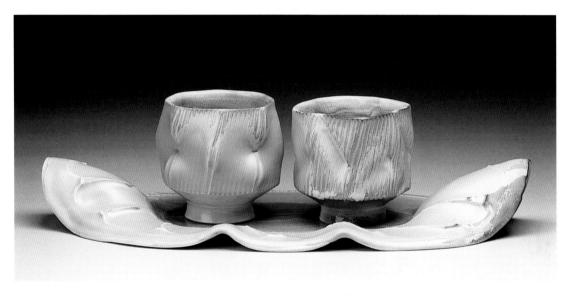

STEVEN ROBERTS
Pink Cups and Tray, 2002

4 x 15 x 6½ in. (10.2 x 38.1 x 16.5 cm)
Thrown and altered porcelain; soda
fired, cone 10
Photo by artist

RITA VARIAN
Untitled, 2003

3 x 3 x 4 in. (7.6 x 7.6 x 10.2 cm)
Slab-built white stoneware; reduction
fired, cone 10
Photo by Leslie Smith

I AM INTERESTED IN THE ABSTRACTION AND EXAGGER-
ATION OF THE FEMALE FIGURE, SINCE ABSTRACTION
CAN BE USED TO TRANSCEND THE RULES REGARDING
CULTURAL IDEALS OF FEMALE BEAUTY. IN A TIME WHEN
WOMEN ARE RARELY AT PEACE WITH THEIR BODIES, I
MAKE WAISTED CUPS, BIRD/WOMAN CREAMERS, AND
WOMBLIKE SUGAR BOWLS TO CELEBRATE THE FEMALE
FORM. BECAUSE THESE FORMS ARE ORGANIC AND
ABSTRACT, THE IMAGERY IS NOT FIXED; THE SAME
FORM MAY SUGGEST AN ANIMAL, A PLANT, OR THE
FEMALE FIGURE TO DIFFERENT VIEWERS.

JOHN GLICK

Mugs, 2003

3¾ x 3 x 3¾ in. (9.5 x 7.6 x 9.5 cm)
Thrown stoneware; reduction fired,
cone 10; glaze painting with wax resist
Photo by artist

GARY HOLT

Loosely Thrown Cup, 2002

4½ x 3 x 3 in.
(11.4 x 7.6 x 7.6 cm)
Wheel-thrown stoneware;
gas fired in reduction,
cone 10; multiple glazes
sprayed under layers of
shino glaze; craze lines
stained with calligraphy
ink; thin spray of yellow
ochre near lip
Photo by Richard Sargent

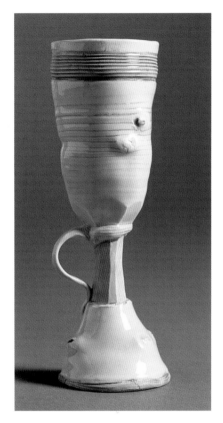

KELLI SINNER
Cups, 2003

4½ x 3 x 3 in. each
(11.4 x 7.6 x 7.6 cm)
Wheel-thrown porcelain;
reduction fired, cone 10;
cobalt slip, trailed dots,
and bisqued stamps
Photo by D. James Dee

GINA FREUEN
Water Goblet, 2003

11 x 4 x 4 in.
(27.9 x 10.2 x 10.2 cm)
Wheel-thrown porcelain,
with coil and slab additions;
gas fired in slight reduction,
cone 6; clear glaze over
colored stains
Photo by Don Hamilton

ROBIN TIEU | 6 x 2¾ x 2¾ in. each
Three Cups, 2002 | (15.2 x 7 x 7 cm)
Slab-built and altered white clay;
electric fired, cone 6
Photo by artist

JAMES TINGEY
Two Cups, 2002

3½ x 8½ x 4 in. each
(8.9 x 21.6 x 10.2 cm)
Thrown and altered porcelain;
wood fired, cone 12; glazed
Photo by Joe Davis

JOSH DeWEESE
Tea Bowls, 2000

Left: 5½ x 4 x 4 in.
(14 x 10.2 x 10.2 cm)
Right: 6 x 4 x 4 in.
(15.2 x 10.2 x 10.2 cm)
Wheel-thrown stoneware;
wood/soda fired; crackle slip
Photo by artist

JEAN NUNEZ DONEGAN | 8 x 4 x 4 in.
Primavera Goblet, 2002 | (20.3 x 10.2 x 10.2 cm)
Hand-built, low-fire, white
body; electric fired, cone 06;
velvet underglazes
Photo by Deborah Lillie

TONY MARTIN
Cup I, 2004

$10\frac{1}{2}$ x 4 x $11\frac{1}{2}$ in.
(26.7 x 10.2 x 29.2 cm)
Hand-built stoneware; electric
fired, cone 06; low-fire glazes
and stains, cone 012
Photo by Julie Hillebrant

MARK FARMER
Rue Christine, 2004

3¾ x 2¾ in. (9.5 x 7 cm)
Thrown porcelain; electric fired,
cone 10; stains and luster, cone 018
Photos by Donald Felton

VLADIMÍR GROH
RADKA LINHARTOVÁ
Untitled, 2001

$4\frac{1}{4}$ x 4 x $3\frac{1}{4}$ in. each
(10.8 x 10.2 x 8.3 cm)
Slip-cast porcelain; gas fired in
reduction, 2408°F (1320°C);
platinum decoration, 1472°F (800°C)
Photo by artists

SUSAN BEINER
Lotus Cup and Saucer, 1999

4½ x 5½ x 5 in. (11.4 x 14 x 12.7 cm)
Slip-cast and assembled porcelain; gas
fired, cone 6; electric fired, cone 04;
luster, cone 018
Photo by Susan Einstein

SARAH PANZARELLA
Teacup and Saucer, 2004

4 x 8 x 3 in.
(10.2 x 20.3 x 7.6 cm)
Wheel-thrown and
altered porcelain; gas
fired in oxidation, cone
9; colored-slip trailing
Photo by artist

9305 LIA TAJCNAR
Untitled, 2003

7 x 5½ x 2 in.
(17.8 x 14 x 5 cm)
Thrown and hand-
built porcelain; raku,
cone 6; electric fired,
cone 10; enamel
Photo by artist

1226A BERNADETTE CURRAN
Animal Hybrids Tumblers, 2003

6 x 3 x 3 in. each (15.2 x 7.6 x 7.6 cm)
Thrown and hand-built porcelain;
electric fired, cone 6; layered colored
slips, terra sigillata, and glazes, cone 6
Photo by Jane G. Miller

JIM KOUDELKA
Coloring Book Cups Set, 2002

8 x 3 x 3 in. each (20.3 x 7.6 x 7.6 cm)
Thrown and incised porcelain; soda
fired, cone 10; various glazes, stains,
and flashing slips
Photo by artist

THESE FUNCTIONAL VESSELS REPRESENT
MY INTEREST AND RESPONSE TO THE
PLASTIC NATURE OF CERAMIC MATERIALS
AND THEIR PROCESS. I REGARD EACH
PIECE AS A PAINTING IN THE ROUND,
WITH THE FORM BECOMING A SCULPTED,
THREE-DIMENSIONAL CANVAS.

JUDITH LEIRE
Espresso Cup and Saucer, 2003

Cup: 1¾ x 3¼ x 2¼ in.
(4.4 x 8.3 x 5.7 cm)
Saucer: ½ x 4 x 2¾ in.
(1.3 x 10.2 x 7 cm)
Slab-built stoneware; gas fired
in reduction, cone 10; olive
celadon glaze
Photo by Joseph Giunta

BURNETA CLAYTON

Small Lavender Cup and Saucer with Dots, 1998

MAKING DOTS BY CUTTING INTO THE SURFACE OF THE DRYING CLAY CAUSES THE GLAZE TO BREAK OVER THEIR EDGES IN THE MELTING FIRE, AND THE FINISHED POT SHOWS FURTHER SUBTLE, LIVELY EVIDENCE OF PROCESS.

3 x 4¼ x 3½ in.
(7.6 x 10.8 x 8.9 cm)
Stoneware; reduction fired, cone 10½
Photo by John Cummings

LISA ALVAREZ BRADLEY

Strawberry/Kiwi Double Dot Cup, 2004

I WANT MY CUPS TO BE AS FLAVORABLE AS THE DRINKS THEY CONTAIN.

3 x 4½ x 3½ in.
(7.6 x 11.4 x 8.9 cm)
Wheel-thrown porcelain; oxidation fired, cone 6
Photo by artist

RICHARD NOTKIN

Barrel on Crate Cup:
Yixing Series, 1994

4⅝ x 5¼ x 2½ in.
(11.7 x 13.3 x 6.4 cm)
Slip-cast, altered, and combined
stoneware; electric fired, cone 6;
celadon glaze interior
Photo by the artist
Courtesy of Garth Clark Gallery,
New York, NY

JEREMY R. BROOKS
Kiln Cup Variation #4, 2002

5 x 3 x 3 in.
(12.7 x 7.6 x 7.6 cm)
Assembled industrial ceramic
materials; electric fired, cones
05 and 11; multi-fired
Photo by artist

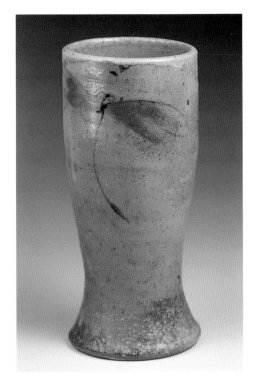

SAM SCOTT
Porcelain Cup with Handle, 2002

4⅝ x 3⅛ in.
(11.7 x 7.7 cm)
Wheel-thrown porcelain;
natural gas fired in
reduction, cone 12;
overglaze brushwork
decoration on clear glaze
Photo by Tom Holt

JOHN ELDER
Tumbler, 2003

6¾ x 3 x 3 in.
(17.1 x 7.6 x 7.6 cm)
Thrown stoneware;
single fired in two-
chamber Noborigama
wood kiln, lightly salted;
slip, brushed decoration
Photo by artist

I ENJOY USING THE DRAGONFLY AS
A DECORATIVE MOTIF. IT ALWAYS
REMINDS ME OF THOSE LONG HOT
SUMMER DAYS AND A COLD DRINK.

GEOFF PICKETT
Untitled Mugs, 2003

$4\frac{1}{2}$ x $3\frac{1}{4}$ x $3\frac{1}{4}$ in.each (11.4 x 8.3 x 8.3 cm)
Thrown porcelain; shino glaze and
brush decoration, cone 10
Photo by Walker Montgomery

ANNETTE GATES
Espresso Shot Cups with Rubies, 2003

2¾ x 2 x 2 in. each (7 x 5 x 5 cm)
Slab-built porcelain; electric fired, cone 6; rubies fired into surface, underglaze wash
Photos by Rob Jackson

CHLOË MARR-FULLER
Two Tumblers, 2003

Left: 5 x 3 x 3 in. (12.7 x 7.6 x 7.6 cm)
Right: 4½ x 3 x 3 in. (11.4 x 7.6 x 7.6 cm)
Wheel-thrown porcelain; gas fired, cone 10;
wax resist, oxide design, and inlay
Photo by Monica Ripley

TYLER BEARD
Celadon Cup, 2004

4 x 3 x 2 in.
(10.2 x 7.6 x 5 cm)
Hand-built stoneware;
oxidation fired, cone 10
Photo by artist

JESSICA DUBIN
Cup and Saucer with Round Handle, 2003

4 x 5 x 4 in.
(10.2 x 12.7 x 10.2 cm)
Wheel-thrown porcelain; gas fired in
reduction, cone 10; iron-saturated glaze
Photo by Howard Goodman

CUPS ARE THE MOST INTIMATE OF OBJECTS. THEY ARE HELD AND
CARESSED DURING USE. THE QUALITIES THAT ATTRACT THE USER—
THE FULLNESS OF FORM, THE FIT AND FEEL OF THE LIP AGAINST
ONE'S OWN, THE COMFORT OF THE HANDLE—ARE THE SAME QUALI-
TIES THAT ARE CONSIDERED BY THE POTTER AS THE CUP IS MADE.
WHAT RESULTS THEN IS A SYMBIOTIC RELATIONSHIP BETWEEN USER
AND MAKER THAT LIVES ON IN THE LIFE OF THE OBJECT ITSELF.

JOANNE TAYLOR BROWN | 6 x 4½ x 3 in.
Shino Cup, 2003 | (15.2 x 11.4 x 7.6 cm)
Slab-built porcelain;
reduction fired, cone 10
Photo by Melissa Enders

BARBARA TIPTON

Cup and Saucer Dreaming (Soft Pillow, Swirled Cup), 2004

4 x 8¾ x 6¼ in.
(10.2 x 22.2 x 15.9 cm)
Hand-built and thrown white clay; electric fired, cone 05; multi-fired, layered slip glaze, cone 05
Photo by artist

BARBARA TIPTON
*Orange Torso (Full-Figured Cup
and Saucer),* 2003

11 x 6¼ x 2½ in.
(27.9 x 15.9 x 6.4 cm)
Electric fired, cone 05; multi-
fired glazes, slip with mica, and
laser-printed decal, cone 05
Photo by artist

DAVID LLOYD WARREN
Tidal Cup, 2004

7 x 3 x 3 in.
(17.8 x 7.6 x 7.6 cm)
Hand-built and low-fire
clay; electric fired, cone
06; enamel accent
Photo by artist

BILLIE JEAN THEIDE
Cups and Trays, 2002

2½ x 8 x 3 in. (6.4 x 20.3 x 7.6 cm)
Hand-built Polish porcelain; gas fired in
reduction, 2516°F (1380°C)
Photo by artist

JOHN WILLIAMS
Map Cups, 2004

THESE CUPS ARE INSPIRED BY
MAPS, PARTICULARLY BY THE TRAN-
SITIONS BETWEEN URBAN AND
RURAL LANDSCAPES.

5 x 3 x 3 in. each
(12.7 x 7.6 x 7.6 cm)
Porcelain; salt and soda fired,
cone 10
Photo by artist

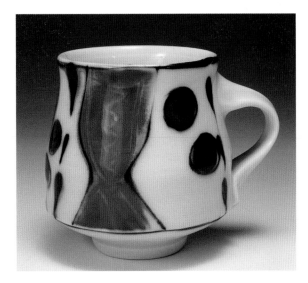

SUSAN FILLEY | 4 x 4 x 3 in.
Mug, 1997 | (10.2 x 10.2 x 7.6 cm)
Thrown porcelain; pulled
handle; reduction, cone 10;
slip decoration
Photo by artist
Decorated by Suze Lindsay

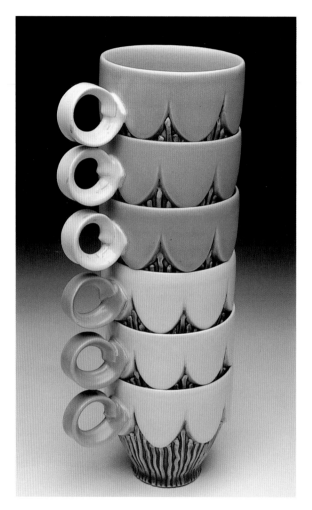

BRENDA QUINN
Six Cups, 2003

10 x 3½ x 3 in.
(25.4 x 8.9 x 7.6 cm)
Thrown and carved porcelain;
gas fired in oxidation, cone 9;
slip trailed
Photo by artist

ZAGROS HATAMI
Three!, 2003

3½ x 5¾ x 4½ in.
(8.9 x 14.6 x 11.4 cm)
Wheel-thrown and hand-built porcelain and earthenware; electric fired,
cone 6; underglaze and clear glaze
Photo by artist

PAULINE PELLETIER
Mug, 2001

3¾ x 4¾ x 3¼ in.
(9.5 x 12 x 8.3 cm)
Cast porcelain; gas fired in reduction,
cone 11; black glaze, bronze, and
copper lusters, cone 018
Photo by C. Jalbert

TARA DAWLEY
Cup and Saucer, 2003

4 x 4½ x 4 in. (10.2 x 11.4 x 10.2 cm)
Wheel-thrown and carved stoneware;
soda fired, cone 10
Photos by E.G. Schempf

THIS FORM WAS DESIGNED SPECIFICALLY TO FEEL GOOD IN THE HAND. THE SQUARE SAUCER WAS ALTERED ON THE EDGE TO CREATE A COMFORTABLE WAVE. THE BOTTOM IS A TACTILE DELIGHT AS WELL AS A VISUAL SURPRISE. THE HANDLE OF THE CUP CURVES OUTWARD ON THE BOTTOM SIDE TO FIT THE CURVE OF A SINGLE FINGER. THE RESULT IS A CUP-AND-SAUCER FORM THAT BECOMES A THOUGHTFUL CHOICE FOR THE USER.

ROBERT "BOOMER" MOORE
Come Along Cup, 2003

6 x 6 x 6 in. (15.2 x 15.2 x 15.2 cm)
Wheel-thrown, assembled, and
altered stoneware; reduction fired,
cone 10; sandblasted
Photo by artist

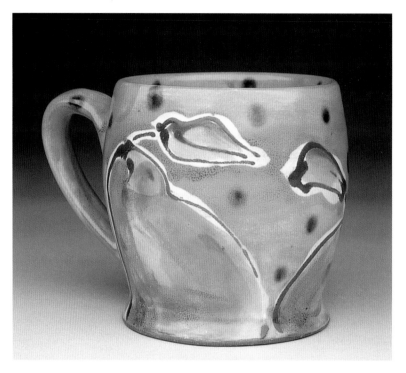

WYNNE WILBUR
Green Pear Cup, 2000

3 x 4½ x 3 in. (7.6 x 11.4 x 7.6 cm)
Wheel-thrown terra cotta; electric
fired, cone 03; majolica
Photo by artist

LINDA ARBUCKLE
Four More Seasons, 2004

$3\frac{1}{2}$ x $4\frac{1}{4}$ x $5\frac{1}{2}$ in.
(8.9 x 10.8 x 14 cm)
Terra cotta; electric
fired, cone 03; majolica
Photo by artist

POSEY BACOPOULOS
Oval Cup, 2002

$4\frac{1}{2}$ x 5 x $2\frac{1}{2}$ in.
(11.4 x 12.7 x 6.4 cm)
Thrown, altered, and assembled terra cotta; electric
fired, cone 04; majolica
Photo by D. James Dee

JAYSON LAWFER
Whiskey Cup Set, 2003

19 x 12 x 4 in. (48.3 x 30.5 x 10.2 cm)
Wheel-thrown porcelain; wood fired
in anagama kiln, cones 10–13; natural
fly ash and glazed exteriors; antique
bottle crate
Photo by Chris Autio

CATHI JEFFERSON
Nine Yonomis, 2003

4 x 3 x 3 in. each (10.2 x 7.6 x 7.6 cm)
Wheel-thrown and altered
stoneware; salt/soda fired
Photo by Hans Sipma

EMILY MURPHY
Yellow Leafy Tumblers, 2003

5½ x 3 x 3 in. each (14 x 7.6 x 7.6 cm)
Wheel-thrown stoneware; soda fired in
oxidation, cone 10; flashing slips
Photo by Guy Nicol

CAROL TOWNSEND
Chair Vessels, 2001

$5\frac{3}{4}$ x $4\frac{1}{2}$ in. each (14.6 x 11.4 cm)
Thrown stoneware; reduction fired,
cone 6; slips and glazes
Photo by artist

LESSONS LEARNED FROM THE SUBTLETY OF MOVEMENT IN NATURE EVENTUALLY FIND THEIR WAY INTO MY WORK. I HAVE ALSO BEEN INFLUENCED BY MY STUDY OF THE INDIGENOUS PAINTED POTTERY OF CRETE AND BY MY VISITS TO THE POTTERY VILLAGES OF MEXICO AND THE PUEBLOS OF THE AMERICAN SOUTHWEST. I AM ALWAYS EAGER TO EXPLORE HOW THE SURFACE PATTERN DEVELOPS A DIALOGUE WITH THE FORM UNDERNEATH.

SARA PATTERSON | 4½ x 3 x 3 in.
Carved Tumbler, 2002 | (11.4 x 7.6 x 7.6 cm)
Thrown and carved porcelain;
gas and soda fired, cone 10
Photo by D. James Dee

VON VENHUIZEN | 4 x 4 x 2½ in.
Cup, 2004 | (10.2 x 10.2 x 6.4 cm)
Wheel-thrown
stoneware; salt fired,
cone 10; slip and glaze
Photo by artist

ROY HANSCOM
Cup #2, 1997

4 x 4 x 5 in.
(10.2 x 10.2 x 12.7 cm)
Thrown stoneware; salt
fired, cone 9
Photo by artist

BRIAN JENSEN
Dimpled Mug, 2003

11 x 5 x 5
(28 x 12.7 x 12.7 cm)
Porcelain; reduction,
cone 10; ash glazes
Photo by artist

BARBARA HOFFMAN
Shino Whiskey Cups, 2003

2½ x 3 x 3 in. each
(6.4 x 7.6 x 7.6 cm)
Wheel-thrown and altered
porcelain; gas fired in reduction,
cone 10; shino glaze
Photo by John Bonath

THE PATTERNS IN THE CARBON TRAP
SHINO GLAZE WERE CREATED BY PLACING
A MESH STYROFOAM OVER THE PIECE
WHILE THE GLAZE DRIED, AND THEN
FIRING THE PIECE IN HEAVY REDUCTION.

BOB NELSON
Two Teadust Cups, 2003

2¾ x 3 in. each (7 x 7.6 cm)
Thrown stoneware; gas/wood fired
in heavy reduction, cone 11;
porcelain slip decoration
Photo by John Bonath

LANA WILSON
Four Functional Cups, 2004

4 x 4½ x 3 in. each
(10.2 x 11.4 x 7.6 cm)
Slab-built white stoneware and
porcelain; electric fired, cone 6;
multiple glazes, cone 04
Photo by artist

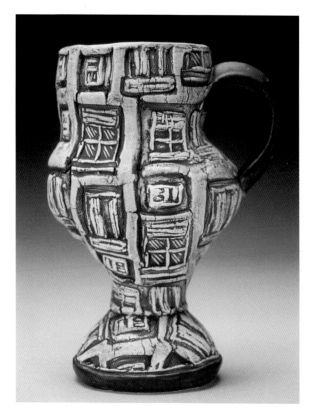

RACHEL BLEIL
Window Mug, 2003

6½ x 5 x 3 in.
(16.5 x 12.7 x 7.6 cm)
Slab-built white earthenware;
electric fired, cone 06; terra
sigillata, stain, and glazes
Photo by artist

DAVID PENDELL
Green Flame Cup, 2001

8¾ x 5¾ x 4 in.
(22.2 x 14.6 x 10.2 cm)
Cast and hand-built earthenware;
electric fired, cone 04; colored
slips; vitreous enamels, cone 018
Photo by artist

BRAD SCHWIEGER
Cup Construction, 2004

14 x 6 x 3 in.
(35.6 x 15.2 x 7.6 cm)
Wheel-thrown and altered
stoneware; soda fired, cone 10;
multiple slips and glazes,
nichrome wire
Photo by artist

YOKO SEKINO
Spineless Love Teacups, 2004

6½ x 6 x 6 in. each
(16.5 x 15.2 x 15.2 cm)
Thrown porcelain; gas fired in
reduction, cone 10; sgraffito
Photo by artist

FARRADAY NEWSOME
Tenderness of Moonlight,
2004

5 x 10 x 10 in.
(12.7 x 25.4 x 25.4 cm)
Thrown terra cotta; electric
fired, cone 5; sgraffito
Photo by artist

JEFF IRWIN
Knotted Cup, 2002

3 x 7 x 7 in. (7.6 x 17.8 x 17.8 cm)
Recycled porcelain cup; electric fired,
cone 03; glaze, sgraffito
Photo by artist

I FIND AN APPROPRIATE CUP AND SAUCER AT
A THRIFT STORE, PAINT IT WITH MY GLAZE,
LET IT DRY, THEN SCRATCH THROUGH THE
UNFIRED GLAZE WITH VARIOUS TOOLS
BEFORE FIRING IT TO CONE 03.

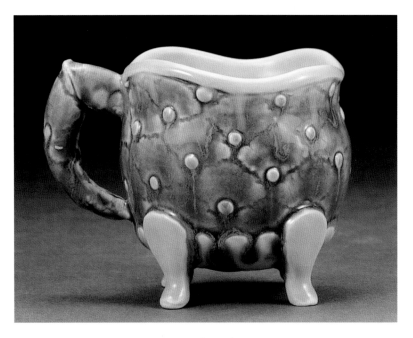

VALERIE DUNCAN
Fugitive Dot Cup, 2003

4 x 4 x 3 in.
(10.2 x 10.2 x 7.6 cm)
Press-molded and slab-built white
stoneware; electric fired, cone 6
Photo by artist

SARA PATTERSON | $3\frac{1}{2}$ x 3 x 3 in. each (8.9 x 7.6 x 7.6 cm)
Pair of Cups, 2002 | Thrown and carved porcelain;
soda/gas fired, cone 10
Photo by D. James Dee

JOSEPH BRUHIN
Tea Bowl Venus, 2003

$3\frac{1}{2}$ x $4\frac{1}{2}$ x $4\frac{1}{2}$ in.
(8.9 x 11.4 x 11.4 cm)
Porcelain; wood fired
Photo by Michael Crow

TONY FERGUSON
#1 Son, 2003

4 x 3¾ x 3¾ in.
(10.2 x 9.5 x 9.5 cm)
Wheel-thrown and altered
stoneware with black granite
and white feldspar; wood fired
in anagama kiln, cone 12; shino,
cobalt, and natural fly ash
Photo by artist

IAN M. SHELLY
Mug, 2004

5 x 5 in.
(12.7 x 12.7 cm)
Stoneware; salt fired,
cone 11
Photo by artist

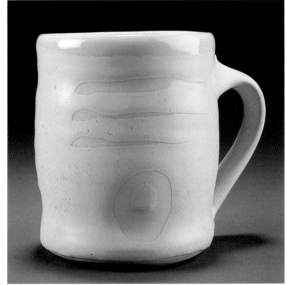

MARIAN BAKER
White Cup, 2003

3½ x 4 x 3 in.
(8.9 x 10.2 x 7.6 cm)
Thrown porcelain; electric
fired, cone 6; glaze, wax resist
Photo by Robert Diamante

LOUISE HARTER
Willow Tree Cup, 2002

3 x 2¾ x 2¾ in.
(7.6 x 7 x 7 cm)
Wheel-thrown stoneware;
wood fired, cone 10;
shino glaze, slip, and
sgraffito decoration
Photo by John Pelverts

TRACY E. SHELL | 6 x 3 x 3 in. each (15.2 x 7.6 x 7.6 cm)
Tumblers, 2004 | Wheel-thrown and altered porcelain;
oxidation fired, cone 6
Photo by artist

JUDITH ARNOLD | 4 x 3 x 3 in. each (10.2 x 7.6 x 7.6 cm)
Spring, 2003 | Thrown earthenware; electric fired,
cone 04; Mason stains; multiple firings
Photo by artist

MIRANDA HOWE
Striped Sake Set, 2003

2½ x 5 x 5 in.
(6.4 x 12.7 x 12.7 cm)
Slab-built porcelain;
salt/soda fired, cone 10
Photo by Dean Adams

BRADLEY KEYS
Scotch for Three, 2004

3½ x 4 x 13 in.
(8.9 x 10.2 x 33 cm)
Thrown and altered red
stoneware; electric fired, cone
6; slips and sprayed glaze
Photo by artist

KAREN SWYLER
Mint Pair, 2003

6 x 11 x 6 in.
(15.2 x 27.9 x 15.2 cm)
Thrown and altered porcelain;
electric fired, cone 10
Photo by artist

LAUREN GALLASPY

Not Your Everyday Nostalgia, 2004

6 x 4 x 4 in.
(15.2 x 10.2 x 10.2 cm)
Slab-built porcelain;
electric fired, cone 6
Photo by Walker Montgomery

AMANDA LYNCH | 9 x 5 in. (22.9 x 12.7 cm)
Untitled, 2003 | Porcelain; soda fired;
underglaze painting
Photo by Ryan Fowler

RACHEL BERG
Tumbler, 2003

5 x 2½ x 2½ in.
(12.7 x 6.4 x 6.4 cm)
Thrown and hand-built
stoneware; soda fired, cone
10; impressed patterns
Photo by artist

TODD HOLMBERG
Cup, 2002

3 x 3¼ x 3¼ in.
(7.6 x 8.3 x 8.3 cm)
Wheel-thrown and altered
stoneware; gas fired in
reduction, cone 10
Photo by Peter Lee

BEN KRUPKA
Mug, 2003

4 x 4 x 3 in.
(10.2 x 10.2 x 7.6 cm)
Wheel-thrown and altered
porcelain; wood fired in
reduction, cone 10
Photo by artist

BRADLEY KEYS
Mug, 2004

4 x 3 x 4 in.
(10.2 x 7.6 x 10.2 cm)
Thrown and altered red
stoneware; electric fired, cone
6; slips and sprayed glaze
Photo by artist

TODD HOLMBERG | 3¾ x 3¼ x 3¼ in.
Square Mug, 2002 | (9.5 x 8.3 x 8.3 cm)
| Wheel-thrown and
altered stoneware;
gas fired in reduction,
cone 10
Photo by Peter Lee

MEIRA MATHISON | 4½ x 3 in. (11.4 x 7.6 cm)
Desert Mug, 2004 | Thrown and altered porce-
lain; cone 10; multi-layered
glazes
Photo by Janet Dwyer

THE NEVADA DESERT COLORS
ARE REFLECTED IN THIS MUG:
LICHEN-LIME GREEN, YELLOW
OCHRE, AND RED AND
YELLOW IRON OXIDE.

KRISTINE HITES
Cold Sake Cup and Saucer, 2003

2⁷⁄₈ x 1¾ x 2¼ in.
(7.3 x 4.4 x 5.7 cm)
Extruded and assembled porcelain;
electric fired in oxidation, cone 6;
glazed and stamped
Photo by Jerry Mathiason

KATHRYNE KOOP
Mug: Blue and Green, 2003

4³⁄₄ x 3¹⁄₄ x 4³⁄₄ in.
(12 x 8.3 x 12 cm)
Wheel-thrown porcelain;
gas fired in reduction,
cone 11; multiple glazes
Photo by Bruce Spielman

TED NEAL

Monarch Cup and Saucer with Bail Handle, 2001

7 x 5 x 5 in.
(17.8 x 12.7 x 12.7 cm)
Wheel-thrown stoneware; wood fired, cones 10–11; steel wire and found objects
Photo by artist

MICHAEL T. SCHMIDT
Two Drink(s), 2003

4½ x 2¾ in. each (11.4 x 7 cm)
Wheel-thrown stoneware; soda
fired, cone 10; nichrome wire
handles; image transfer, cone 06
Photo by artist

JOAN PEVARNIK
Caught, 2003

4 x 12 x 7 in. (10.2 x 30.5 x 17.8 cm)
Thrown stoneware; salt fired,
cone 10; mixed media
Photo by Martha Lochert

JIM KOUDELKA
Coffee Stop Cup, 2001

THIS PIECE REFERENCES MY LOVE
OF AND ADDICTION TO COFFEE.

7 x 14 x 6 in. (17.8 x 35.6 x 15.2 cm)
Thrown, molded, hand-built, and
assembled stoneware; salt fired, cone
10; multiple low-fire glazes, cone 06;
metal chain; sandblasted
Photo by artist

JESSICA M. STOLLER
Asymmetrical Hair Cups, 2003

I HAVE ALWAYS COLLECTED PICTURES OF
UNIQUE AND ONE-OF-A-KIND HAIRSTYLES; THEY
FASCINATE ME. WHEN I SEE GOOD HAIR, I NOT
ONLY COMPLIMENT IT, I MAKE WORK ABOUT IT.

3 x 3½ x 3 in. each (7.6 x 8.9 x 7.6 cm)
Slip-cast porcelain; cone 6; silkscreened
photo decals, cone 018
Photos by artist

MANDY WOLPERT
The Bathers, 2004

$3\frac{1}{2}$ x 9 x $3\frac{3}{4}$ in. (8.9 x 22.9 x 9.5 cm)
Thrown and hand-built earthenware;
underglazes, clear glaze
Photo by Greg Piper

DAVID PENDELL

Flame Cup: Fire and Ice Series, 2000

$7\frac{1}{2}$ x $4\frac{3}{4}$ x $2\frac{3}{4}$ in. (19 x 12 x 7 cm)
Hand-built and cast earthenware;
electric fired, cone 04; vitreous
enamels and luster, cone 018
Photo by artist

WOLFGANG VEGAS
Coffee Cocktail, 2003

7 x 4¾ x 6 in.
(17.8 x 12 x 15.2 cm)
Slip-cast earthenware;
electric fired, cone 03;
glazed
Photo by François Ruegg

LISA KARMAZIN
Cup and Saucer, 2001

5 x 6 x 4 in. (12.7 x 15.2 x 10.2 cm)
Wheel-thrown and slab-built porcelain;
oxidation fired, cone 6
Photo by David Harrison

KAREN NEWGARD | 4 x 4 x 4 in. each (10.2 x 10.2 x 10.2 cm)
Mugs, 2004 | Wheel-thrown porcelain; salt fired,
cone 10; terra sigillata, sgraffito
Photo by Walker Montgomery

BECKY LLOYD
Tea Bowl with Leaves, 2003

$3\frac{1}{2}$ x $3\frac{1}{2}$ x $3\frac{1}{2}$ in.
(8.9 x 8.9 x 8.9 cm)
Wheel-thrown porcelain;
salt fired, cone 10; sgraffito
on black terra sigillata
Photo by Peter Lee

NATALIE KASE
Two Cups, 2004

3 x 3½ x 3½ in. each
(7.6 x 8.9 x 8.9 cm)
Hand-built white stoneware; gas
fired in reduction, cone 10; glazed
interior, rutile wash exterior
Photo by Joseph Giunta

NAOKO GOMI
Cylinder Cups: Turtle Motif, 2003

5 x 2½ x 2½ in. each
(12.7 x 6.4 x 6.4 cm)
Slab-built colored porcelain;
electric fired, cone 9
Photo by artist

BILL GRIFFITH
Tumblers, 2003

7 x 2¾ x 2¾ in. each
(17.8 x 7 x 7 cm)
Slab-built stoneware;
soda fired, cone 10; embossed
Photo by Jeff Brown

CHRIS GUSTIN
Set of Tumblers, 2002

6 x 3 x 3 in. each (15.2 x 7.6 x 7.6 cm)
Wheel-thrown porcelain; wood/soda
fired, cone 11
Photo by Dean Powell

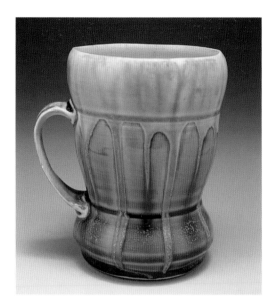

RYAN J. GREENHECK | 5½ x 5½ x 3½ in.
Handled Cup, 2003 | (14 x 14 x 8.9 cm)
Wheel-thrown porcelain;
wood fired, cone 10
Photo by artist

MISSY M. McCORMICK | 4½ x 4½ x 3½ in.
Spray Green Cup, 2003 | (11.4 x 11.4 x 8.9 cm)
Wheel-thrown stoneware;
soda fired, cone 10
Photo by artist

SCOTT PLACE
Cup Form, 2002

4 x 4 x 3 in.
(10.2 x 10.2 x 7.6 cm)
Thrown and altered
stoneware; wood
fired, cone 10
Photo by artist

TYLER BEARD
Wood Cups, 2003

$4^{1}/_{2}$ x 3 x 3 in. each
(11.4 x 7.6 x 7.6 cm)
Hand-built and wheel-thrown
stoneware; wood fired, cone 10
Photo by artist

I WAS INSPIRED BY THE RELIC
QUALITY OF DILAPIDATED
BARNS ON THE EAST COAST.

JARED BRANFMAN
Cup on Tray, 2003

7 x 7 in. (17.8 x 17.8 cm)
Thrown, gouged, and altered
stoneware; wood fired,
cone 10; ash glaze
Photo by artist
Courtesy of Charles Moore

GARY HOLT
Square Faceted Cup, 2002

$3\frac{1}{2}$ x $3\frac{1}{2}$ x $3\frac{1}{2}$ in.
(8.9 x 8.9 x 8.9 cm)
Wheel-thrown and faceted
stoneware; reduction fired,
cone 10; multiple glazes
sprayed under thick shino;
craze lines stained with calligraphy ink; thin spray of yellow
ochre to promote iridescence
Photo by Richard Sargent

JIL FRANKE
Teacup, 2004

$3\frac{1}{2}$ x 3 x 3 in.
(8.9 x 7.6 x 7.6 cm)
Slab-built stoneware; wood
fired in double-chamber
Bourry box kiln, cone 10;
slip decorated
Photo by Kirk Lyttle

RIMAS VISGIRDA
Picasso Cup, 1995–1997

6 x 8 x 8 in. (15.2 x 20.3 x 20.3 cm)
Extruded and slab-built stoneware;
electric fired, cone 10; glaze and
underglaze pencil, cone 05; lusters
and china paints, cone 017
Photo by artist

SUZE LINDSAY
Set of Tumblers, 2004

7 x 3¾ x 3¾ in. each
(17.8 x 9.5 x 9.5 cm)
Thrown stoneware; salt fired, cone 10
Photo by Tom Mills

SANDI PIERANTOZZI
Tumblers, 2003

Tallest: 6 x 3 x 3½ in.
(15.2 x 7.6 x 8.9 cm)
Wheel-thrown, carved porcelain;
wood fired, cone 11; slips
Photo by artist

GEORGE HANDY

Stack of Cups, 2003

EACH PIECE IS SPONTANEOUSLY PAINTED;
MY PROCESS IS VERY FREE, MUCH LIKE
FUSION JAZZ.

4 x 4 in. each (10.2 x 10.2 cm)
Slip-cast porcelain; electric fired,
cone 7; stains over clear glaze
Photo by Tim Barnwell

DANIEL GEGEN
Spiral Cups, 2003

5½ x 5 x 2½ in. each
(14 x 12.7 x 6.4 cm)
Hand-built stoneware; gas fired,
cone 5; saggar-fired terra sigillata
Photo by artist

CAROL GOUTHRO
Cups, 2004

3 x 6 x 3 in. each
(7.6 x 15.2 x 7.6 cm)
Slip-cast and hand-built terra cotta;
electric fired, cones 04–05; hand-
painted underglazes, clear glaze
Photo by artist

C. PARKER ROBINSON | $3\frac{1}{2}$ x $2\frac{1}{2}$ x $2\frac{1}{2}$ in. each (8.9 x 6.4 x 6.4 cm)
Pair of Face Cups, 1998 | Wheel-thrown porcelain; gas fired with salt,
cone 10; sgraffito design
Photo by Walker Montgomery

LAURA JEAN McLAUGHLIN
Little Red Wine Glass, 2003

SURREALISTIC METHODS OF AUTOMATIC
INSPIRATION WERE USED IN THE CONSTRUC-
TION AND EMBELLISHMENT OF THIS CUP.

8 x 3 x 3 in.
(20.3 x 7.6 x 7.6 cm)
Slip-cast porcelain; electric fired,
cone 7; slips, glaze, sgraffito
Photo by Michael Ray

PAUL SCOTT
Scott's Cumbrian Blue(s),
Cup No. 1, 2003

4¾ x 6 x 2 in. (12 x 15.2 x 5 cm)
Slab-built porcelain; electric, cones 5–6;
slip, screenprinted decal
Photo by artist

IAN C. ANDERSON
Ian Eats the World!, 2004

3¾ x 3¼ x 3¼ in. each
(9.5 x 8.3 x 8.3 cm)
Slip-cast white earthenware;
electric fired; ceramic decals
Photo by artist

SABINE MOSHAMMER
Cup with Newspaper Print, 2000

$3\frac{1}{2}$ x $3\frac{1}{2}$ x $3\frac{1}{2}$ in. (8.9 x 8.9 x 8.9 cm)
Thrown stoneware; gas fired, cones 7
and 11; colored slip, on-glaze print
Photos by artist

CAROLE HANSON
Lace Series, 2004

Left: 4½ x 3½ x 3½ in.
(11.4 x 8.9 x 8.9 cm)
Right: 4 x 3½ x 3½ in.
(10.2 x 8.9 x 8.9 cm)
Slip-cast porcelain and stoneware;
electric fired in oxidation, cone 10;
copper red glaze
Photo by artist

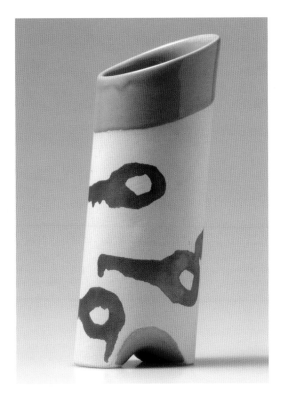

DIMITAR PETROV PETROV
Series Cup: The New World I, 2003

6 x 2¼ x 2¼ in.
(15.2 x 5.7 x 5.7 cm)
Gypsum-cast porcelain; electric fired,
2156°F (1180°C); decals, 1427°F
(775°C); painted with feather
Photo by Vasil Germanov

JASON HESS
Three Tea Bowls, 2003

5½ x 3 x 3 in. each
(14 x 7.6 x 7.6 cm)
Stoneware; wood fired with soda
Photo by artist

MATT LONG
Whiskey Cups, 2003

4 x 4 in. each (10.2 x 10.2 cm)
Porcelain; soda fired, cone 11
Photo by artist

PEG MALLOY
Three Wood-Fired Mugs, 2001

4 x 4 x 3¼ in. each
(10.2 x 10.2 x 8.3 cm)
Wheel-thrown and faceted
porcelain; wood fired, cone 11
Photo by artist

STEPHEN GRIMMER

Three Bourbon Cups on Stand, 2003

6 x 16 x 5$\frac{1}{2}$ in. (15.2 x 40.6 x 14 cm)
Wheel-thrown stoneware; reduction
fired, cone 10; inlaid slip and glazes
Photo by artist

LINDA KLIEWER
Squared Serving Cups, 2003

Cups: 4 x 3½ x 2 in. each (10.2 x 8.9 x 5 cm)
Tray: 4 x 12¼ x 5½ in. (10.2 x 31.1 x 14 cm)
Thrown and slab-built porcelain cups and
stoneware tray; electric fired, cone 5
Photo by Courtney Frisse

SHANE M. KEENA | 21 x 9 x 9½ in.
Porifera Cup, 2004 | (53.3 x 22.9 x 24.1 cm)
Wheel-thrown, hand-
built, and slip-cast porcelain with stoneware base;
electric fired, cone 6;
additional firings, cone 04
Photo by David Calicchio

SCOTT PLACE | 7 x 5 x 4 in.
Cup Form, 2002 | (17.8 x 12.7 x 10.2 cm)
Thrown and altered
stoneware; wood fired,
cone 10
Photo by artist

LESLEY BAKER
Dear Stein, 2002

REFERENCING HISTORICAL PORCELAIN, I
MOLD, CAST, AND ASSEMBLE OBJECTS
FROM MY LIFE AND DISPLAY THEM AS
PERSONAL TROPHIES.

8 x 6 x 4 in. (20.3 x 15.2 x 10.2 cm)
Slip-cast and assembled porcelain;
electric fired, cone 6
Photo by artist

STEVEN ROBERTS
Two Tea Bowls, 2003

3$\frac{1}{2}$ x 3$\frac{1}{2}$ in. each (8.9 x 8.9 cm)
Thrown and altered porcelain;
soda fired, cone 10
Photo by artist

JOHN WILLIAMS | 5 x 3 x 3 in. each (12.7 x 7.6 x 7.6 cm)
Map Cups, 2004 | Porcelain; salt/soda fired, cone 10
Photo by artist

ELIZABETH FLANNERY
Juice Cups, 2003

3 x 2$\frac{1}{2}$ x 3 in. each
(7.6 x 6.4 x 7.6 cm)
Wheel-thrown stoneware; gas fired in
reduction, cone 10; inlaid and layered
slips, fake ash glaze
Photo by John Polak

MICHAEL CONNELLY
Tumblers, 2004

6 x 3 x 3 in. each (15.2 x 7.6 x 7.6 cm)
Wheel-thrown white stoneware; soda
fired, cone 10
Photo by artist

MICHAEL MAGUIRE | 3 x 3 x 3 in. each (7.6 x 7.6 x 7.6 cm)
Whiskey Cups, 2004 | Wheel-thrown stoneware; salt fired,
cone 10; sprayed and brushed oxides
Photo by artist

ANGELA K. HUNG
Square Cup, 2003

3½ x 2¼ x 4½ in.
(8.9 x 5.7 x 11.4 cm)
Wheel-thrown and altered
porcelain; salt/soda fired,
cone 10
Photo by Jeff Burce

ROBIN DUPONT
Mug, 2003

4½ x 3 x 3 in.
(11.4 x 7.6 x 7.6 cm)
Thrown stoneware;
wood fired, cone 12
Photo by Rita Taylor

JUDITH DUFF
*Wood-Fired Yonomi (Cup
for Everyday Use)*, 2003

4 x 3 x 3 in.
(10.2 x 7.6 x 7.6 cm)
Wheel-thrown and altered
porcelain; wood fired, cone
12; natural ash glaze
Photo by Tom Mills

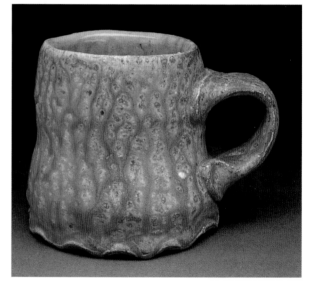

LAUREL MacDUFFIE
Cup, 2004

$3\frac{1}{2}$ x $4\frac{1}{2}$ x 3 in.
(8.9 x 11.4 x 7.6 cm)
Wheel-thrown stoneware;
salt fired, cone 10
Photo by artist

DALE HUFFMAN | 3 x 3 in. (7.6 x 7.6 cm)
Cup, 2003 | Wheel-thrown porcelain;
wood fired, cone 12; applied
and natural ash glaze
Photo by artist

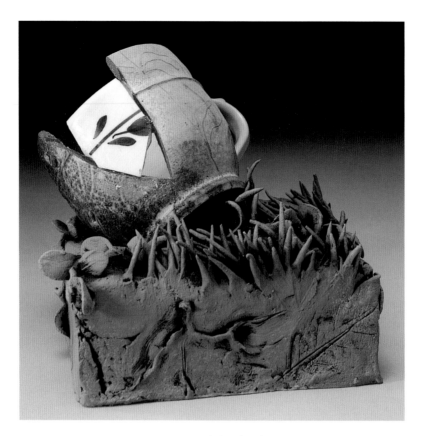

SUSAN BOSTWICK
A Slice of Life, 2001

MUCH OF MY WORK IS INSPIRED BY
WHAT IS BENEATH OUR FEET, FROM A
SIMPLE ARRANGEMENT TO THE DRAMA
OF TRANSFORMATION. SHARDS FOUND
ON WALKS THROUGH THE WOODS (DIS-
CARDED REMNANTS FROM PREVIOUS
GENERATIONS) WERE THE SEEDS FOR
THIS CUP-AND-SAUCER SERIES.

6 x 6 x 6 in. (15.2 x 15.2 x 15.2 cm)
Press-molded, modeled, and thrown
earthenware; electric fired, cone 04;
multiple-fired slips, stains, and glazes
Photo by Joseph Gruber

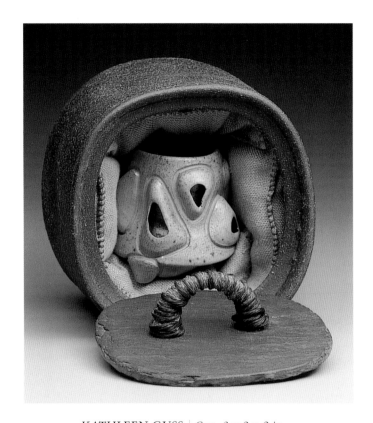

KATHLEEN GUSS
STEPHEN ROBISON
Scotch Cup and Box, 2003

Cup: 3 x 2 x 2 in.
(7.6 x 5 x 5 cm)
Box: 5 x 5 x 5 in.
(12.7 x 12.7 x 12.7 cm)
Thrown and hand-built stoneware;
wood/soda fired in reduction, cone 10
Photo by Stephen Robison

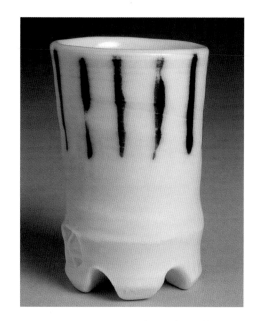

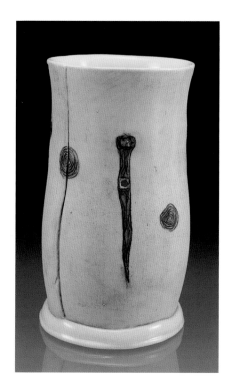

KIRK LYTTLE
Shot Cup, 2002

2¼ x 1½ x 1½ in.
(5.7 x 3.8 x 3.8 cm)
Thrown Southern Ice
porcelain; fired in double-
chamber Bourry box kiln,
cone 10; commercial
underglaze decoration
Photo by artist

ROB JACKSON
ANNETTE GATES
Cup with Nails, 2004

4 x 2 x 2 in. (10.2 x 5 x 5 cm)
Slab-built porcelain; electric
fired, cone 6; glass and
faceted sapphires fired into
porcelain, underglaze washes
Photo by Rob Jackson

JOSEPH LYON
Oil Filter Cups, 2002

Left: 6 x 3½ x 3½ in.
(15.2 x 8.9 x 8.9 cm)
Right: 4¼ x 3½ x 3½ in.
(10.8 x 8.9 x 8.9 cm)
Slip-cast porcelain; soda fired
in reduction, cone 10
Photo by artist

SARAH HEIMANN
Two Cups, 2001

3¾ x 5 in. each (9.5 x 12.7 cm)
Carved white stoneware; salt fired, cone
6; layered slips and glaze
Photo by Peter Lee

KURT BRIAN WEBB | 5½ x 6 x 6 in. (14 x 15.2 x 15.2 cm)
Bird Watcher, 2004 | Pinched stoneware; soda fired
Photo by artist

GEOFF CALABRESE | 10 x 6 x 4 in.
Cup and Saucer, 2003 | (25.4 x 15.2 x 10.2 cm)
Coil-built stoneware; salt fired,
cone 2; terra sigillata
Photos by Walker Montgomery

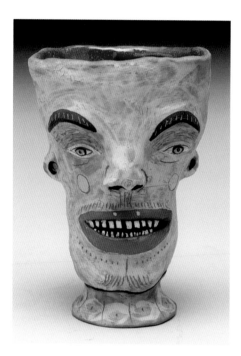

JENNY MENDES
Toothy Two-Faced Cup, 2002

4¾ x 3 x 3 in.
(12 x 7.6 x 7.6 cm)
Coil-built earthenware;
electric fired, cone 02;
terra sigillata; black
wash over incised lines
Photo by Heather Protz

SHIGERU MIYAMOTO
Tropicopolitan Drinking Vessel, 1999

8½ x 6¼ x 4¼ in.
(21.6 x 15.9 x 10.8 cm)
Coil-built stoneware; pit fired
Photos by Brad Goda

LAUREN GALLASPY

Mid-Morning Jester, Afternoon Augur, 2004

$3^{1/2}$ x $3^{1/2}$ x 2 in.
(8.9 x 8.9 x 5 cm)
Slab-built porcelain; electric
fired, cone 6
Photo by Walker Montgomery

I WOULD LIKE MY VESSELS, AS FUNCTIONAL FORMS THAT NECESSITATE PHYSICAL CONTACT, TO ENCOURAGE AN INTERACTION THAT MIRRORS INTIMATE ENGAGEMENT BETWEEN HUMANS. I HOPE TO CREATE A WORLD THAT IS BOTH ACCESSIBLE AND MYSTERIOUS, ONE THAT ALLOWS THE USER IN, THOUGH NEVER COMPLETELY. IDEALLY, MY CUPS MAY SPEAK TO THEIR AUDIENCE IN A SORT OF CONSPIRATORIAL WHISPER, WHILE GIVING AWAY A FEW OF THEIR SECRETS—NOT OUT OF A HERMETIC SENSE OF PRIVACY, BUT RATHER, FROM A COMMITMENT TO PRESERVING THE UNKNOWN AND UNKNOWABLE.

ULTIMATELY, EACH PIECE CAN BE SEEN AS AN EFFORT TO RECREATE WHAT I FIND SO COMPELLING IN EVERYDAY EXISTENCE, THAT WHICH I MAY MEET WITH GENUINE WONDER: THE UNASSUMINGLY ARTICULATE, THE UNEXPECTEDLY ATTRACTIVE, THE DISCREETLY DIVINE.

RIMAS VISGIRDA
A Cup and Its Shadow,
1995–1997

6 x 8 x 8 in.
(15.2 x 20.3 x 20.3 cm)
Extruded and slab-built
stoneware; electric fired,
cone 10; glaze and under-
glaze, cone 05; lusters and
china paints, cone 017
Photo by artist

ANN TUBBS
Titanium Face Mug, 2002

5 x 5½ in. (12.7 x 14 cm)
Thrown and altered clay; electric
fired, cone 2; majolica
Photo by Jerry Anthony

I AM FASCINATED BY THE HUMAN FACE
AND BY THE RANGE OF EMOTIONS INDI-
CATED IN THE LINES OF EYES, NOSE,
AND MOUTH. I'M ALSO INTERESTED IN
HOW THE MOVEMENT OF THE FIRING
CHANGES WHAT I HAVE PERCEIVED IN
MY ORIGINAL PAINTING.

LINDA ARBUCKLE
Wide Red with Fruit, 2004

3¼ x 4¾ x 6 in.
(8.3 x 12 x 15.2 cm)
Terra cotta; electric fired,
cone 03; majolica
Photo by artist

FARRADAY NEWSOME
*Yellow Cup and Saucer with
Oranges and Grapes,* 2002

5 x 10 x 10 in.
(12.7 x 25.4 x 25.4 cm)
Thrown terra cotta; electric
fired, cone 5; majolica
Photo by artist

ROSALIÉ WYNKOOP
Cups, 2002

4 x 4½ x 3¼ in. each
(10.2 x 11.4 x 8.3 cm)
Tin-glazed terra cotta; electric fired,
cone 03; gold luster, cone 018
Photo by Josh DeWeese

JEREMY M. KANE
Mustache Series, 2004

5 x 5 x 5 in. each (12.7 x 12.7 x 12.7 cm)
Hand-built and thrown porcelain;
reduction fired, cone 10; decals
and luster, cone 018
Photos by artist

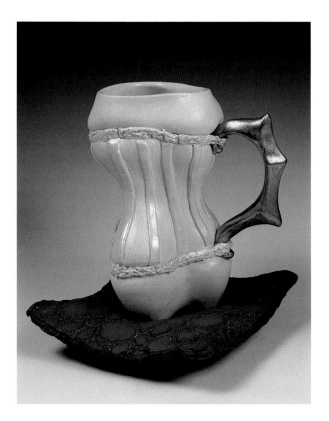

TERESA SHANNON
Corseted Cup on Pillow Saucer, 2003

9 x 5 x 5 in.
(22.9 x 12.7 x 12.7 cm)
Hand-built and slip-cast white and red earthenware; electric fired, cone 04; gold and mother-of-pearl lusters, cone 020
Photo by artist

CAROL GOUTHRO
Cup with Pleated Skirt, 2004

7 x 5 x 3 in.
(17.8 x 12.7 x 7.6 cm)
Slip-cast and hand-built earthenware; underglazes, glazes, lusters, cones 04–05
Photo by Roger Schreiber

197

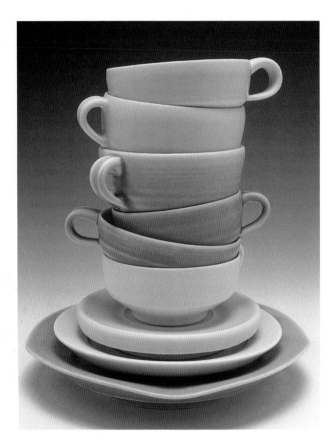

BENJAMIN SCHULMAN
Stacked Teacup Set, 2004

8 x 6 x 6 in. (20.3 x 15.2 x 15.2 cm)
Wheel-thrown porcelain; electric
fired, cone 6
Photo by artist

DAVID PIER | $3\frac{3}{4}$ x 4 x $4\frac{1}{4}$ in. each
Coffee Cups, 2004 | (9.5 x 10.2 x 10.8 cm)
Slip-cast porcelain; electric
fired, cone 10
Photo by artist

SUSAN DOUGLASS
Tea Bowls, 2003

3½ x 4 x 4 in. each (8.9 x 10.2 x 10.2 cm)
Wheel-thrown and paddled porcelain
with sprig decoration; reduction fired,
cone 10; clear glaze
Photo by artist

THERESA PUFFER
Rudy, 2004

$4^{1}/_{2}$ x $5^{1}/_{4}$ x 3 in.
(11.4 x 13.3 x 7.6 cm)
Wheel-thrown earthenware; electric
fired, cone 03; underglaze and glaze
Photo by Peter Lee

KEVIN L. TURNER
Solenopsis Pair, 2003

8 x 8 x 5 in. each
(20.3 x 20.3 x 12.7 cm)
Hand-built and slip-cast porcelain;
reduction fired, cone 10; glazed
and sanded surface
Photo by artist

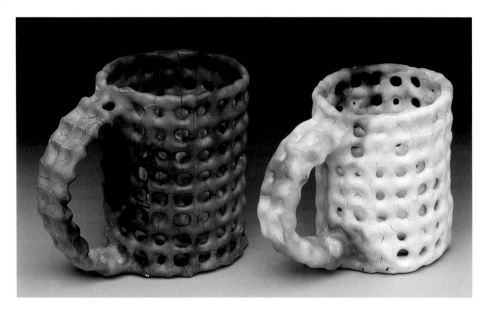

LINDA HANSEN MAU
Two Mugs, 2003

4 x 5 x 3 in. each
(10.2 x 12.7 x 7.6 cm)
Porcelain paper clay on steel wire;
electric fired, cone 04; terra sigillata;
smoked in open tub with newspaper
Photo by Lynn Hunton

ERIK TRAGUS
Faceted Cup, 2003

$4\frac{1}{4}$ x $3\frac{1}{4}$ x $3\frac{1}{4}$ in.
(10.8 x 8.3 x 8.3 cm)
Wheel-thrown and faceted
porcelain; anagama fired, cone
12; Malcolm's Shino glaze
Photo by Jim Walker

XIAO YUN WANG
Shino Tea Bowl, 2003

2¾ x 3¼ x 3¼ in. (7 x 8.3 x 8.3 cm)
Wheel-thrown porcelain; anagama fired,
cones 11–12; Malcolm's Shino glaze
Photo by Jim Walker
Collection of Alice C. Sabatini Gallery,
Topeka, KS

JENNIFER LAWLER-MECCA
Teacup and Saucer, 2004

4 x 3 x 5½ in.
(10.2 x 7.6 x 14 cm)
Thrown and altered
porcelain; electric fired,
cone 7; stamped, stained
Photo by artist

MICHÈLE C. DRIVON
Teacup, 2003

5 x 6 in. (12.7 x 15.2 cm)
Wheel-thrown porcelain;
oxidation fired, cone 6
Photo by Robert Gibson

DEBORAH SCHWARTZKOPF
Cup and Saucer, 2003

3 x 6 in. (7.6 x 15.2 cm)
Wheel-thrown earthenware;
electric fired, cone 02
Photo by artist

LESLIE NORTON
Squared Teacup with Saucer, 2003

4 x 6 x 6 in. (10.2 x 15.2 x 15.2 cm)
Wheel-thrown and altered white
stoneware; reduction, cone 10; sprayed
and dipped glazes
Photo by artist

THE TEACUP OR MUG IS MY MOST PERSONAL
LINK TO THE PEOPLE WHO USE MY POTTERY.
MORE TIME IS SPENT WITH A TEACUP OR
MUG THAN ANY OTHER TYPE OF POTTERY.
IT'S USUALLY A TIME OF REFLECTION AND
INNER THOUGHT OR PERHAPS IT'S SPENT
WITH A SPECIAL FRIEND.

LESLEY BAKER
Interlock, 2001

7 x 6 x 5 in.
(17.8 x 15.2 x 12.7 cm)
Slip-cast and assembled porcelain;
reduction fired, cone 6
Photo by artist

SHAWN L. PANEPINTO
Teatle Cups, 2004

9 x 26 x 16 in. each (22.9 x 66 x 40.6 cm)
Wheel-thrown and hand-built earthenware;
electric fired, cone 06; multi-fired with
low-fire lithium glazes and underglazes
Photo by Tony Rinaldo

ENZIEN KUFELD
Ice Crystal Liquor Cups, 2003

$2\frac{3}{4}$ x $2\frac{1}{4}$ x $2\frac{1}{4}$ in. each
(7 x 5.7 x 5.7 cm)
Wheel-thrown stoneware; wood/soda fired,
cone 12; high-alumina slip
Photo by Christian D. Barr

**LINDSAY
WIECZOREK**
Tumbler Set, 2004

$5\frac{1}{2}$ x $2\frac{1}{2}$ in. each
(14 x 6.4 cm)
Thrown stoneware;
soda fired, cone 10
Photo by John Lucas

JAMES TINGEY
Three Tumblers, 2002

I TRY TO PRODUCE A RANGE OF
SURFACE TONES, RECORDING THE FLAME
THAT UNIQUELY NUANCES EACH PIECE.

6 x 13 x 4 in. each (15.2 x 33 x 10.2 cm)
Thrown and slipped stoneware;
salt fired, cone 10
Photo by Joe Davis

CHRISTIAN D. BARR | 6 x 3½ x 5 in. each (15.2 x 8.9 x 12.7 cm)
Beer Steins, 2003 | Wheel-thrown stoneware; wood/soda
fired, cone 12; reed slip decoration,
Helmar slip
Photo by artist

CHRIS "ARNY" ARENSDORF
Highball Cups, 2003

3½ x 3 x 3 in. each
(8.9 x 7.6 x 7.6 cm)
Wheel-thrown porcelain;
wood/soda fired, cone 11
Photo by artist

McKENZIE SMITH
Coffee Cups, 2003

3 x 3 x 3 in. each (7.6 x 7.6 x 7.6 cm)
Thrown stoneware; soda fired, cone 10
Photo by artist

MARILYN DENNIS
PALSHA
Duet Cup, 2001

4 x 4¾ x 3 in.
(10.2 x 12 x 7.6 cm)
Thrown stoneware; gas
fired with salt and soda,
cone 10; slip brushwork
Photo by Seth Tice-Lewis

SCOTT K. ROBERTS
Mug, 2003

4 x 4 in. (10.2 x 10.2 cm)
Wheel-thrown stoneware;
gas fired, cone 10; salt
glazed, single fired
Photo by Bret West

AMY E. SMITH
Parlour Player, 2004

9 x 8 x 8 in. each
(22.9 x 20.3 x 20.3 cm)
Hand-built stoneware; reduction
fired, cone 10; crackle slip and
celadon glaze
Photo by artist

GEO LASTOMIRSKY

Cup #4, 1996

$3^5/8$ x $5^1/2$ x $5^1/2$ in. (9.2 x 14 x 14 cm)
Thrown and hand-built terra cotta;
electric fired, cone 04; terra sigillata,
cone 04
Photo by Tom Holt

IS IT THE POT THAT FORMS THE POTTER?

217

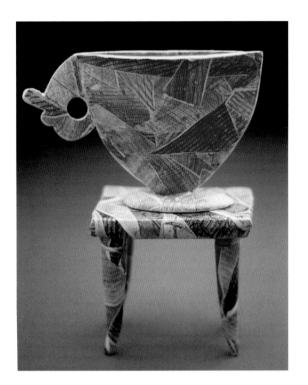

BARBARA
CHADWICK-BLAND
*Patchwork Cup with
Stand*, 2000

8 x 6 x 3 in.
(20.3 x 15.2 x 7.6 cm)
Hand-built porcelain;
electric fired, cone 9;
monoprint collage with
underglazes and clear glaze
Photo by artist

DAVID CUZICK
*Homage to the
Cup*, 2003

7 x 4 x 4 in.
(17.8 x 10.2 x 10.2 cm)
Wheel-thrown
stoneware; gas fired in
reduction, cone 10;
sprayed with artificial
salt glaze and oxides
Photo by artist

SHELDON GANSTROM
Bathsheba Smiles, 2002

31 x 16 x 6 in. (78.7 x 40.6 x 15.2 cm)
Slab and wheel-thrown stoneware;
electric and raku fired, cone 8
Photo by artist

CYNTHIA SIEGEL
Spiral Ceremonial Cup, 2001

I BELIEVE THAT FRESH, INNOVATIVE WORK
RESULTS FROM CONTINUAL EXPLORATION
AND DEVELOPMENT. I SEE MY COMMIT-
MENT TO CLAY AS A REFLECTION OF MY
LIFE'S JOURNEY, IN WHICH I COMBINE MY
APPRECIATION FOR THE NATURAL WORLD
AND ITS CULTURES WITH DAILY ARTISTIC
AND CREATIVE GROWTH.

5 x 4 in. (12.7 x 10.2 cm)
Wheel-thrown and carved white
stoneware; electric fired in oxidation,
cone 8; layered copper glazes
Photo by Stan Einhorn and artist

JOHN A. ULERY
Bottoms Up Cup, 2003

THE SIDE DESIGN WAS ACTUALLY WHAT
WAS LEFT ON THE WHEEL HEAD AFTER I
LINE-CUT THE CUP.

3$\frac{1}{2}$ x 4 x 4 in.
(8.9 x 10.2 x 10.2 cm)
Wheel-thrown and assembled
white stoneware; salt and
soda fired, cone 10
Photo by Sarah L. Rossiter

CAROL ANN WEDEMEYER
Cup, 2002

6 x 5 x 4½ in.
(15.2 x 12.7 x 11.4 cm)
Coil-built and slab-built
Arctic White porcelain;
fired twice, cone 5
Photo by Wilfred J. Jones

THIS PIECE IS VERY LIGHTWEIGHT,
WITH EVEN WALL THICKNESS, AS I
HAVE STUDIED THE CRAFT OF
HAND BUILDING FOR MANY YEARS.
IT WAS DESIGNED WITH FUNCTION
IN MIND, FEATURING A KNUCKLE
NICHE FOR THE USER.

JARED WARD
Cup, 2003

5 x 4 x 3 in.
(12.7 x 10.2 x 7.6 cm)
Wheel-thrown and extruded porcelain; gas fired in oxidation, cone 9;
sprayed glazes
Photo by artist

CRAIG EDWARDS
Cup and Saucer Duet, 2004

THE DUALIST DANCE OF LIFE WAS THE
INSPIRATION FOR THIS SET.

4 x 5½ x 5½ in.
(10.2 x 14 x 14 cm)
Slab-built porcelain;
electric fired, cone 8
Photo by Peter Lee

KARIN SOLBERG | 4 x 3 x 3 in. each (10.2 x 7.6 x 7.6 cm)
Cups, 2003 | Thrown and altered porcelain; salt
fired, cone 11; inlaid slips with glaze
Photo by artist

RUCHIKA MADAN
Pair of Cups, 2003

4 x 4½ x 4 in. each (10.2 x 11.4 x 10.2 cm)
Wheel-thrown stoneware; oxidation
fired, cone 6; sgraffito
Photo by artist

CHRISTIAN D. BARR
Water Cup, 2003

5 x 3 x 3 in.
(12.7 x 7.6 x 7.6 cm)
Wheel-thrown and
altered stoneware;
wood/soda fired, cone 12
Photo by artist

STEPHEN FOEHNER
Yonomi, 2003

4 x 4 x 4 in.
(10.2 x 10.2 x 10.2 cm)
Wheel-thrown stoneware;
gas fired in reduction, cone
9; carbon trap shino glaze
and copper flashing
Photo by Forrest Doud

JIM CONNELL
Red Carved Cup, 2003

$5\frac{1}{2}$ x $3\frac{1}{2}$ x $3\frac{1}{2}$ in.
(14 x 8.9 x 8.9 cm)
Thrown and carved porcelain;
reduction fired, cone 10
Photo by artist

CAROLE HANSON
Winter Series, 2004

Left: 2¾ x 3¼ x 3¼ in.
(7 x 8.3 x 8.3 cm)
Right: 2½ x 3¼ x 3¼ in.
(6.4 x 8.3 x 8.3 cm)
Thrown Southern Ice porcelain; electric
fired in oxidation, cone 10; clear and
copper red glazes
Photo by artist

MICHÈLE C. DRIVON | 5 x 6 in. (12.7 x 15.2 cm)
Teacup 2003 | Wheel-thrown porcelain;
oxidation fired, cone 6
Photo by Robert Gibson

JUDITH PAPIAN | 3¼ x 3¼ in.
Gingko Cup with | (8.3 x 8.3 cm)
Cut Rim, 2004 | Thrown, cut, and incised
translucent porcelain;
reduction fired, cone 10
Photo by Tony Deck

PETER BATTAGLENE
Cup, 2004

4 x 3½ x 3½ in.
(10.2 x 8.9 x 8.9 cm)
Thrown Limoges porcelain; gas
fired in reduction, cone 11; paper
stencils, water-etched decoration
Photo by Peter Whyte

VLADIMÍR GROH
RADKA LINHARTOVÁ
Untitled, 2001

$4\frac{1}{4}$ x 4 x $3\frac{1}{4}$ in.
(10.8 x 10.2 x 8.3 cm)
Slip-cast porcelain; gas fired in
reduction, 2408°F (1320°C); platinum decoration, 1472°F (800°C)
Photo by artists

SANDRA TORRES
Tall Cups, 2003

6 x 2 in. (15.2 x 5 cm)
Thrown and altered porcelain; gas
fired, cone 10; cobalt sulphate
exterior, clear glaze interior
Photo by artist
Collection of Paula Purcell

I AIM TO EXPLORE THE BEAUTY OF PORCELAIN,
ITS SHAPE, ITS COLOR, AND ITS FEELING.

VELIMIR VUKIĆEVIĆ
Spiral, 2003

2¾ x 3¾ x 3¼ in.
(7 x 9.5 x 8.3 cm)
Slip-cast, bone-china
porcelain; electric fired,
cone 10; drawing gum
resist
Photo by Vlada Popović

LISA M. JOHNSON
Cupload-a Creamers, 2003

6⅛ x 10 x 6⅝ in.
(15.5 x 25.4 x 16.8 cm)
Earthenware; electric fired,
cone 8; raku; satin matte
white, cone 04; individual
creamers slipped together
to form cup
Photo by Jeff Sabo

233

DEBORAH J. WEINSTEIN
Blue Spotted Mugs, 2003

5 x 3½ in. each (12.7 x 8.9 cm)
Thrown and altered stoneware;
cone 6; underglaze, glaze
Photo by Robert Nelson

LISA KARMAZIN
Cup and Saucer, 2001

4 x 7 x 3½ in.
(10.2 x 17.8 x 8.9 cm)
Wheel-thrown and
carved porcelain;
oxidation fired, cone 6
Photo by David Harrison

HEESEUNG LEE
Pedestal Tumblers 2004

7 x 3 x 3 in. each (17.8 x 7.6 x 7.6 cm)
Slab-built and cast terra cotta; electric
fired, cone 1; Xerox transfer, luster,
and decals, cone 018
Photo by John Carlano

JUDITH PAPIAN
Gingko Cups and Tray, 2003

I AM INSPIRED BY NATURE: THE AUTUMN
GROUND LITTERED WITH GINKO FANS,
THE LAYERED FOOTHILLS OF VIRGINIA
VIEWED FROM A DISTANCE, THE
TRANSLUCENT BLUE-GREEN SEA.

3½ x 10½ x 6½ in.
(8.9 x 26.7 x 16.5 cm)
Thrown, slab-built, and incised
porcelain; reduction fired, cone 10
Photo by Tony Deck

THERESA M. GRESHAM
Leaf Cup 2, 2004

4 x 7 x 7 in. (10.2 x 17.8 x 17.8 cm)
Thrown and hand-built porcelain;
electric fired, cone 6; rutile wash
under clear glaze
Photo by Rocky Lewycky

SHARON D. MORRIS
Zen Circle Teacup, 2003

3 x 4 x 2¾ in. (7.6 x 10.2 x 7 cm)
Wheel-thrown porcelain; bisque, cone 06; glazes, cone 10; layered glazes with wax-resist brushwork
Photo by Ken Sanville

HIDE SADOHARA
Untitled, 2003

3½ x 3 x 3 in. each (8.9 x 7.6 x 7.6 cm)
Wheel-thrown porcelain; wood fired, cone 11
Photo by artist

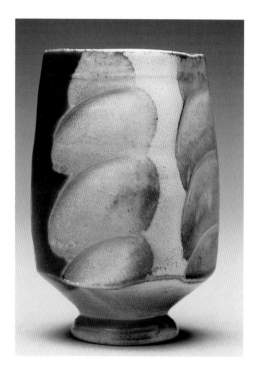

CONNIE CHRISTENSEN
Shino Mug, 2002

5 x 4 x 3 in.
(12.7 x 10.2 x 7.6 cm)
Wheel-thrown porcelain;
reduction fired, cone 10;
shino glaze
Photo by John Bonath,
Maddog Studio

SALLY CAMPBELL
Sipping Cup, 2002

2½ x 2 x 2 in.
(6.4 x 5 x 5 cm)
Thrown and altered
porcelain; wood/salt
fired, cone 10; flashing
slip and glazes
Photo by Mike Cady

I USE PORCELAIN BECAUSE OF ITS
ABILITY TO CAPTURE AND RECORD
THE SMALLEST, SUBTLEST
DETAILS, PROJECTING ITS LUMI-
NOUS QUALITIES THROUGH SLIPS
AND GLAZES. WOOD AND SALT
FIRING FURTHER ENHANCES THE
NUANCES OF THE MATERIAL.

KATHY PHELPS | $4\frac{1}{4}$ x 5 x $2\frac{3}{4}$ in.
Something's Fishy, 2001 | (10.8 x 12.7 x 7 cm)
Wheel-thrown and altered
stoneware; soda fired,
cone 10; slip decoration
Photo by Walker Montgomery

SCOTT K. ROBERTS | $3\frac{1}{2}$ x $3\frac{1}{2}$ in. (8.9 x 8.9 cm)
Yonomi, 2003 | Wheel-thrown stoneware;
gas fired, cone 10; salt
glazed, single fired
Photo by Bret West

POSEY BACOPOULOS
Lattice Cups, 2003

4 x 4½ x 3 in. each
(10.2 x 11.4 x 7.6 cm)
Thrown terra cotta; electric fired,
cone 04; majolica
Photo by Kevin Noble

SHELBY DUENSING
Raku Tea Bowl, 2003

3 x 3½ x 3½ in.
(7.6 x 8.9 x 8.9 cm)
Wheel-thrown stoneware;
propane-fueled raku kiln,
cone 06; post-fired reduction
with newspaper
Photo by Rocky Lewycky

CAROLINE CERCONE | 3 x 3 x 3½ in.
Yonomi Teacup, 2004 | (7.6 x 7.6 x 8.9 cm)
Thrown stoneware; gas
fired in reduction, cone
10; layered shino, ash
glaze, wax resist, and
slip application
Photo by artist

MICHAEL ORGAN
Landscape Cup, 2003

4½ x 6 x 4½ in.
(11.4 x 15.2 x 11.4 cm)
Hand-built earthenware,
stoneware, and porce-
lain; electric fired, cone
10; brushed glazes with
metal oxides
Photo by artist

IN GENERAL, A CUP IS A SMALL
ROUND DRINKING VESSEL. BUT
IT CAN ALSO BE A PRIZE FOR
SPORT, A CALYX IN A PLANT, A
SOCKET IN A BONE. MY CUPS
ARE A MEANS OF DISTILLING
AND TRANSFORMING VISUAL
AND HAPTIC EXPERIENCES OF
SPECIFIC LANDSCAPES INTO
COMMONPLACE VESSEL FORMS.

JOHN SELLBERG
*Cups on Wall-Mounted
Base #3*, 2003

6 x 12 x 5 in.
(15.2 x 30.5 x 12.7 cm)
Hand-thrown stoneware;
wood fired, cone 12
Photo by John Lucas

LYN SMITH BERNSTEIN
Raku Cup with Applications, 2004

5 x 4 x 4¾ in. (12.7 x 10.2 x 12 cm)
Wheel-thrown and altered white
stoneware; bisque, cone 07; raku,
cones 07–08; crash-cooled crackle glaze
and reduced crackle slip
Photo by artist

BONNIE SEEMAN | 5½ x 4½ x 4½ in.
Untitled, 2004 | (14 x 11.4 x 11.4 cm)
| Wheel-thrown and altered porcelain;
| electric fired, cone 10
| Photo by artist

SARAH PANZARELLA
Teacup and Saucer, 2004

3½ x 8 x 3 in. (8.9 x 20.3 x 7.6 cm)
Wheel-thrown and altered porcelain;
gas fired in oxidation, cone 9
Photo by artist

THADDEUS POWERS
Cup and Saucer, 2004

PATTERN IS VERY IMPORTANT IN MY
WORK. THE FLUIDITY OF A PATTERN
OVER A FORM HELPS DESCRIBE ITS SHAPE.
DEPENDING ON SCALE AND GLAZES USED,
I CAN BRING THE SHAPE TO THE FORE-
GROUND WITH PATTERN, OR MASK THE
SHAPE UNTIL IT NEARLY DISAPPEARS.

$4\frac{1}{4}$ x $5\frac{3}{4}$ in.
(10.8 x 14.6 cm)
Thrown porcelain; salt
fired in neutral, cone
10; applied slip
Photo by artist

BERNADETTE CURRAN
Raccoon Island Tumblers, 2003

6 x 3 x 3 in. (15.2 x 7.6 x 7.6 cm)
Thrown and hand-built porcelain; electric fired, cone 6; layered colored slips,
terra sigillata, and glazes, cone 6
Photo by artist

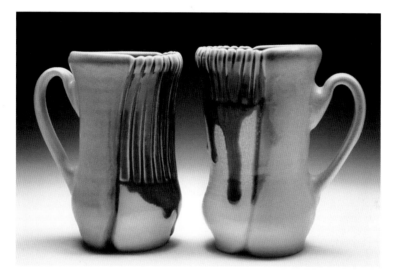

LeANNE ASH
Carved Cups, 2003

5½ x 4½ x 3 in. each
(14 x 11.4 x 7.6 cm)
Wheel-thrown porcelain; salt
fired, cone 10; glaze
Photo by artist

MARY E. BRIGGS
Bird Pondering Bug, 2003

3½ x 4¾ in. (8.9 x 12 cm)
Wheel-thrown terra cotta;
electric fired, cone 04
Photo by Joe Davis

RANDY HINSON
Teacup, 2002

3 x 4 x 3 in.
(7.6 x 10.2 x 7.6 cm)
Wheel-thrown stoneware;
salt fired, cone 10
Photo by Lynn Ruck

NAN COFFIN
I'm Seeing Spots #1, 2003

3 x 5 x 4 in.
(7.6 x 12.7 x 10.2 cm)
Wheel-thrown porcelain;
downdraft gas fired in
reduction, cone 10
Photo by Richard Burkett

RITA J. VALI
Cup on Pedestal, 2004

7 x 5 in. (17.8 x 12.7 cm)
Wheel-thrown and altered white
stoneware; electric fired in oxidation,
cone 6; multiple layers of colored
slip, sgraffito
Photo by artist

FLEUR SCHELL
Porcelain Cup, 2001

5¼ x 4½ in. (13.3 x 11.4 cm)
Wheel-thrown and assembled
porcelain; electric fired, 2327°F
(1275°C); acrylic resist, cobalt
carbonate inlay
Photo by artist

GILLES LE CORRE
Two Tea Bowls, 2002

3¾ x 3½ x 3 in. each
(9.5 x 8.9 x 7.6 cm)
Hand-thrown and altered stoneware;
gas fired in reduction, cone 10
Photo by Chris Honeywell

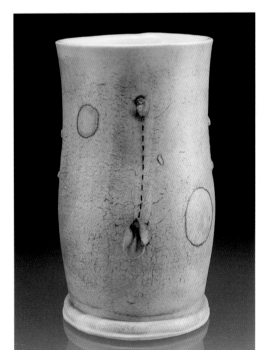

ANNETTE GATES
Wine Cup, 2003

4 x 2¼ x 2½ in.
(10.2 x 5.7 x 6.4 cm)
Slab-built porcelain;
cone 6; fused glass
inlay, underglaze wash
Photo by Rob Jackson

LYNN SMISER BOWERS
Set of Mugs, 2004

4½ x 3¾ x 2¾ in. each (11.4 x 9.5 x 7 cm)
Wheel-thrown porcelain; gas fired in
reduction, cone 10; stencils, wax resist,
and oxide brushwork
Photo by E.G. Schempf

BARBARA TIPTON
Cup Drawing, 2002

$3\frac{1}{2}$ x $7\frac{1}{2}$ x 6 in. (8.9 x 19 x 15.2 cm)
Hand-built and thrown white stoneware;
electric fired, cone 05; multiple firings;
laser-printed decal, cone 05
Photos by artist

I BEGAN THIS CUP THE WAY I MAKE OVAL
DISHES—THROWING AND ALTERING A
BOTTOMLESS CYLINDER. I LET THE DRAW-
ING RUN DOWN THE SIDE AND ADDED A
HANDLE, HOPING FOR A PLAY BETWEEN
TWO AND THREE DIMENSIONS. THE DECAL
ON THE SIDE IS FROM AN ALCHEMY TEXT,
BECAUSE CERAMICS IS ALCHEMY.

TIM LUDWIG
Cup with Walnuts, 2003

5½ x 6 x 3 in.
(14 x 15.2 x 7.6 cm)
Thrown and altered
earthenware; electric
fired, cone 04; slips
with Mason stains
Photo by Bede Clarke

BONITA COHN
Autumn, 2003

$3\frac{3}{8}$ x $4\frac{3}{4}$ x $2\frac{3}{4}$ in.
(8.6 x 12 x 7 cm)
Wheel-thrown stoneware;
fired in anagama kiln,
cone 12; shino slip and
natural flashing
Photo by artist

SO OFTEN IN ANAGAMA
FIRINGS, THE PIECES LOOK
LIKE THE COLORS OF THE
SEASON IN WHICH THEY
WERE FIRED.

CARY JOSEPH
Orange Cup For Tea, 2003

$3\frac{1}{2}$ x 3 x 3 in. (8.9 x 7.6 x 7.6 cm)
Wheel-thrown and altered white
stoneware; gas fired in reduction,
cone 10
Photo by David Orser

TONY FERGUSON | 3¾ x 3¾ x 3¾ in.
Crab, 2003 | (9.5 x 9.5 x 9.5 cm)
Wheel-thrown and altered
stoneware with black granite
and white feldspar; wood
fired in anagama kiln, cone
12; shino and natural fly ash
Photo by artist

PHILLIP S. AHNEN | 3 x 5 x 5 in.
Firebox Cup with Drip, 2003 | (7.6 x 12.7 x 12.7 cm)
Wheel-thrown stoneware;
wood fired, cone 12
Photo by Peter Lee

KRISTIN BENYO
Square Mug, 2004

4½ x 5 x 3½ in. each (11.4 x 12.7 x 8.9 cm)
Thrown and altered stoneware; electric
fired, cone 6; glaze, wax resist
Photo by artist

JUSTYNA K. BENTON
Wine Glasses, 2004

$3\frac{1}{4}$ x $3\frac{1}{4}$ x $3\frac{1}{4}$ in. each (8.3 x 8.3 x 8.3 cm)
Slip-cast, colored porcelain; soda-vapor
fired, cone 10
Photo by artist

MARGARET PATTERSON
Windowed Tumblers, 2003

5 x 2½ x 2½ in.
(12.7 x 6.4 x 6.4 cm)
Thrown and altered stoneware;
gas fired in reduction, cone 10
Photo by Bart Kasten

ANNETTE GATES
Cappuccino Cup, 2003

3 x 2½ x 3 in.
(7.6 x 6.4 x 7.6 cm)
Slab-built porcelain; electric
fired, cone 6; fused-glass inlay,
underglaze wash
Photo by Rob Jackson

LIZ GARRETT
Juice Glasses/Cups, 2003

4 x 3 in. each (10.2 x 7.6 cm)
Wheel-thrown porcelain; gas fired in
reduction, cone 10; layered glazes
Photo by Steve Sauer

GARY JACKSON

Soda-Textured Temmoku, 2004

5 x 3½ x 4¾ in.
(12.7 x 8.9 x 12 cm)
Wheel-thrown stoneware;
soda fired, cone 10; hand-stamped details
Photo by Guy Nicol

GEORGIA TENORE JADICK

Mug, 2004

A SPECIAL CUP CAN BE JUST
AS UPLIFTING AS THE WARM
LIQUID INSIDE IT.

4 x 3½ x 3 ¼ in.
(10.2 x 8.9 x 8.3 cm)
Wheel-thrown stoneware;
reduction; shino glaze, wax
painted, sponged glazes
Photo by artist

KERI LOGEL

Butter Yellow Mug with Saucer, 2004

5 x 3 x 4½ in. (12.7 x 7.6 x 11.4 cm)
Wheel-thrown and slab-built
porcelain; electric fired, cone 10;
square and line imprints
Photo by artist

YAEL NOVAK
Tea Time, 2003

Cup: 3½ x 4¼ in. (8.9 x 10.8 cm)
Tray: 8¾ x 5¼ in. (22.2 x 13.3 cm)
Wheel-thrown stoneware; slab-built tray;
oxidation, cone 7; wax resist decoration,
glaze, and underglaze
Photo by Ilan Amihai

WALTER BROWN | 5½ x 3 in. (14 x 7.6 cm)
Thrown and Paddled | Thrown and paddled
Tumbler, 2003 | white stoneware; wood
fired, cone 12
Photo by John Lucas

MATT LONG | 6½ x 3 in.
Victory Tumbler, 2004 | (16.5 x 7.6 cm)
Porcelain; soda
fired, cone 11
Photo by artist

BARRY CARPENTER
Two Cups, 2002

7 x 2½ x 2½ in. each
(17.8 x 6.4 x 6.4 cm)
Wheel-thrown porcelain;
wood fired, cone 12
Photo by artist

JEFF GORDON
Untitled, 2004

2⅞ x 4¾ x 3⅞ in.
(7.3 x 12 x 9.8 cm)
Hand-built earthenware; electric
fired; bisque, cone 04, glaze
cone 06; luster, cone 019
Photo by Kevin Downey

RITA VARIAN
Untitled, 2003

3 x 4 x 3 in. each (7.6 x 10.2 x 7.6 cm)
Slab-built white stoneware; reduction
fired, cone 10
Photo by Leslie Smith

MIRANDA HOWE
Three Cups, 2003

3 x 2½ x 2½ in. each (7.6 x 6.4 x 6.4 cm)
Slab-built porcelain; salt and
soda fired, cone 10
Photo by Dean Adams

MARK STROM
Shino Glazed with a Twist, 2003

5 x 3¼ x 3¼ in.
(12.7 x 8.3 x 8.3 cm)
Thrown and faceted porcelain;
gas fired, cone 10; shino and
sifted ash glaze
Photo by Tom Holt

FACETING THIS PIECE AND THEN
STRETCHING IT WITH FURTHER
THROWING ACCENTUATED ITS
MOVEMENT AND MADE IT APPEAR
TO ALMOST DANCE.

ROY HANSCOM
Cup #1, 1997
5 x 5 x 4 in. (12.7 x 12.7 x 10.2 cm)
Thrown stoneware;
salt fired, cone 9
Photo by artist

JILL LAWLEY
Tilting Cups, 2003

4½ x 3½ in. each
(11.4 x 8.9 cm)
Thrown and altered light
stoneware; terra sigillata; wood
fired, cone 10
Photo by artist

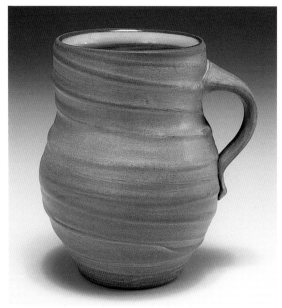

PAUL LINHARES
Shapely Mug, 2003

4 x 3½ x 2¾ in.
(10.2 x 8.9 x 7 cm)
Wheel-thrown earthen-
ware; electric fired,
cone 5; thick slip and
terra sigillata
Photo by artist

LAURA MOORE
Mug, 2002

3 x 4 x 3½ in.
(7.6 x 10.2 x 8.9 cm)
Porcelain; pine fired
Photo by artist

RICHARD NOTKIN | Dice Cup: 3⅛ x 2⅞ x 2⅞ in. (7.7 x 7.3 x 7.3 cm)
Set of Three Cups, 1993 | Crate Cup: 3⅜ x 3⅜ x 3½ in. (8.6 x 8.6 x 8.9 cm)
Cube Skull Cup: 3⅛ x 2⅞ x 2⅞ in. (7.7 x 7.3 x 7.3 cm)
Slip-cast, altered, and combined stoneware;
electric fired, cone 6; celadon glaze interior
Photo by artist
Courtesy of Garth Clark Gallery, New York, NY

MELISSA MENCINI
Paper Cup, 2003

1³⁄4 x 4 x 3¹⁄2 in. (4.4 x 10.2 x 8.9 cm)
Slab-built porcelain; gas fired, cone
10; liner underglaze application
Photo by artist

SIGRID K. ZAHNER
Cup, 2004

5½ x 5 x 3 in.
(14 x 12.7 x 7.6 cm)
Slip-cast porcelain and
press-molded stoneware;
electric fired, cone 04;
clear glaze, stain
Photo by Wilbur Montgomery

THE BODY OF THE CUP IS MADE
FROM AN OLD PAIR OF RIBBED
TIGHTS THAT WERE STUFFED AND
TIED WITH STRING. I ADDED
DETAIL BY SEWING ON ODD
THINGS, SUCH AS BUTTONS AND
SCREWS. THEN I MADE A PLASTER
MOLD OF THAT, CAST IT, AND
ADDED A HANDLE, RIM, AND FOOT.

IAN STAINTON
Cup, 2003

5 x 4¼ in. (12.7 x 10.8 cm)
Thrown stoneware; reduc-
tion fired, cone 10; separat-
ing glaze over black slip
Photo by Harry Holder

SARAH MYERSON
Blue Flicked Cup, 2002

THIS PIECE WAS INSPIRED BY DELICATE
AND TRANSLUCENT FORMS, SUCH AS
PETALS. I WORK SPONTANEOUSLY,
RESPONDING TO THE DIFFERENT WAYS
THAT CLAY CAN BE MANIPULATED.

2 x 2¾ x 2¾ in. (5 x 7 x 7 cm)
Flicked and extruded porcelain;
electric fired, 1260° C
Photo by Nigel Essex

DOUG SCHRODER
Food-Stamp Cup, 2004

5½ x 3 x 3 in.
(14 x 7.6 x 7.6 cm)
Wheel-thrown stoneware;
soda fired, cone 10
Photos by artist

A SUCCESSFUL VESSEL SHOWS
THE MARK AND STRESS OF THE
FIRE, RECORDING THE SURVIVAL
OF A TRAUMATIC EVENT.

TED NEAL
*Cup and Saucer with
Bail,* 1998

6 x 5 x 5 in.
(15.2 x 12.7 x 12.7 cm)
Stoneware; soda fired;
sandblasted; steel wire
Photo by Jeff Bruce

TOSHIKO K. CARNAL
Oil Spot Teacup, 2004

2¾ x 3½ x 3½ in.
(7 x 8.9 x 8.9 cm)
Wheel-thrown porcelain;
oxidation fired in downdraft
propane gas kiln, cone 10
Photos by John Lucas

CHERYL WOLFF
Teacup, 2004

3½ x 3 in. (8.9 x 7.6 cm)
Wheel-thrown white
stoneware; oxidation fired,
cone 9; layered glazes
Photo by George Post

SUZE LINDSAY
Two Mugs, 2003

$4^{1}/2$ x 3 x 3 in. each
(11.4 x 7.6 x 7.6 cm)
Thrown and altered stoneware;
salt fired, cone 10
Photo by Tom Mills

LEA ZOLTOWSKI
Bubble Cups, 2003

4½ x 3½ x 3 in. each
(11.4 x 8.9 x 7.6 cm)
Hand-built porcelain;
oxidation, cone 10
Photo by artist

COLLETTE SMITH
Square Mug with Feet,
2003

4 x 3 x 4 in.
(10.2 x 7.6 x 10.2 cm)
Thrown and altered porce-
lain; gas fired in reduction,
cone 10; dipped JB Shino
glaze, sprayed oribe glaze
over rutile; brushwork
accent
Photo by Joe Guinta

AFTER SO MANY YEARS OF
ROUND POTS, SQUARES
AND OVALS ARE EXCITING.
I NEVER KNOW WHAT
WILL APPEAR!

REENA KASHYAP
Morning Tea, 2004

4 x 4½ x 2½ in.
(10.2 x 11.4 x 6.4 cm)
Wheel-thrown porcelain;
gas fired in reduction,
cone 10; Gustin Shino
glaze with iron oxide
and black stain brush
decoration
Photo by Joe Giunta

THE CARBON TRAPPING IN
SHINO GLAZES IS A GIFT OF THE
KILN. I ALWAYS USE IT BECAUSE
OF ITS UNPREDICTABILITY.

LIZ SPARKS | 5 x 3 in. each (12.7 x 7.6 cm)
Mugs, 2003 | Wheel-thrown stoneware;
methane gas fired, cone 9
Photo by Tom Mills

MARSHA KARAGHEUSIAN
Dad, Tea, and Me, 2003

STEEPED IN A 400-YEAR-OLD
TRADITION, THE RAKU-FIRED
TEACUP REMAINS A VIABLE ART
FORM WORTHY OF FURTHER
EXPLORATION AND DISCOVERY.

4½ x 4 x 4 in.
(11.4 x 10.2 x 10.2 cm)
Thrown and trimmed raku;
raku fired, cone 011; glazed
Photo by Eric Workum

AL TENNANT
T Bowl, 2003

4 x 4 in. (10.2 x 10.2 cm)
Wheel-thrown porcelain;
wood fired in anagama kiln,
cone 13; reduction cooled,
cone 07; shino crackle exterior,
shino glaze interior
Photo by Steve Sauer

GERTRUDE GRAHAM SMITH
Tea Bowls, 2003

THE PRIMARY FOCUS OF MY WORK IS MAKING
OBJECTS OF BEAUTY FOR PEOPLE TO USE AND
ENJOY. HOW DOES ONE CHOOSE A MORNING COF-
FEE CUP...BY THE WAY YOUR HAND CRADLES THE
WARM CUP, HOW THE RIM OF THE CUP MEETS
YOUR LIPS? I STRIVE TO MAKE MY POTTERY TAC-
TILE, VISUALLY INTRIGUING, AND PLEASURABLE,
WITH AN ORDINARY BEAUTY THAT ENHANCES,
NOURISHES, AND ENRICHES DAILY LIFE.

4 x 4 x 4 in. each (10.2 x 10.2 x 10.2 cm)
Wheel-thrown and faceted porcelain;
soda fired, cone 10
Photo by Tom Mills

MYRA KAHA
Mug, 2004

3¼ x 3¼ x 2¾ in.
(8.3 x 8.3 x 7 cm)
Porcelain; soda fired,
cone 10
Photo by artist

SARAH DUNSTAN
Porcelain Cup 2003

2¾ x 2½ in. (7 x 6.4 cm)
Slab-built porcelain;
electric, cone 9
Photo by Steve Tanner

JESSICA DONNELL
Untitled, 2004

3¼ x 5½ x 4 in.
(8.3 x 14 x 10.2 cm)
Thrown porcelain; electric
fired, cone 6
Photo by artist

SKUJA BRADEN
Composition with Cups, 2003

Largest: 6¼ x 3¼ in. (15.9 x 8.3 cm)
Hand-built porcelain; gas fired in
reduction, cone 11; celadon, shino,
and temmoku glazes
Photo by Angela Braden

MARIE J. PALLUOTTO
Untitled, 1999

5 x 3 x 4½ in.
(12.7 x 7.6 x 11.4 cm)
Wheel-thrown, altered,
and stamped porcelain;
reduction fired, cone 10
Photo by Ken Woisard

JEFF REICH
Sculptural Cups, 2004

6 x 3 x 6 in.
(15.2 x 7.6 x 15.2 cm)
Wheel-thrown and altered
stoneware; gas fired in
reduction, cone 10; torn
tape and wax resist, glaze
Photo by artist

TRACY E. SHELL | 7 x 3 x 3 in.
Tumbler, 2004 | (17.8 x 7.6 x 7.6 cm)
Wheel-thrown porcelain;
oxidation fired, cone 6
Photo by artist

LEE REXRODE
Nesting, 2003

THE GREEN BASE IS ACTUALLY A
HOLLOW TUBE. A SMALLER CUP
WAS MADE AND INSERTED INSIDE,
THEN THE TWO PARTS WERE FUSED
TOGETHER WITH THE GLAZE.

5¾ x 4½ x 3¼ in.
(14.6 x 11.4 x 8.3 cm)
Wheel-thrown porcelain; salt
fired, cone 10; brushed oxides
Photo by artist

SANDRA DAULTON
SHAUGHNESSY

Striper Cup, 2004

$4\frac{1}{8}$ x $4\frac{1}{2}$ x $3\frac{1}{2}$ in.
(10.5 x 11.4 x 8.9 cm)
Wheel-thrown white stoneware;
soda fired, cone 10; flashing
slip, glaze, and underglaze
Photo by Karen Brown

SALLY CAMPBELL
Sipping Cup, 2002

$2\frac{1}{2}$ x 2 x 2 in.
(6.4 x 5 x 5 cm)
Thrown and altered
porcelain; wood/salt
fired, cone 10; slip
and glazes
Photo by Mike Cady

CHRIS LONGWELL
Cup, 2003

4 x 4 x 4 in.
(10.2 x 10.2 x 10.2 cm)
Wheel-thrown stoneware;
soda fired, cone 10
Photo by artist

BETHANY BENSON
Cup and Saucer, 2002

5¼ x 4⅛ x 2¾ in.
(13.3 x 10.5 x 7 cm)
Thrown and altered white
stoneware; soda fired, cone
10; black slip decoration
with glaze
Photo by artist

RUCHIKA MADAN | 4 x 5 x 4 in.
Blue Mug, 2003 | (10.2 x 12.7 x 10.2 cm)
Wheel-thrown white stoneware;
oxidation fired, cone 6; sgraffito
Photo by artist

WILLIAM BAKER
Two Small Cups, 2004

$3\frac{1}{2}$ x 3 x 3 in. each
(8.9 x 7.6 x 7.6 cm)
Wheel-thrown and carved porcelaneous stoneware; salt and soda fired, cone 10; kaolin slip, applied ash
Photo by artist

RAY CHEN
Life II, 2003

4 x 5½ x 5 in.
(10.2 x 14 x 12.7 cm)
Wheel-thrown and slab-built
stoneware; wood fired in reduction,
cone 10; white slip on surface
Photo by Mark Rockwood

BRENDA QUINN | 4 x 6 x 4 in.
Slit Mug, 2002 | (10.2 x 15.2 x 10.2 cm)
Thrown and altered porcelain;
wood fired, cone 10
Photo by artist

STEVEN GODFREY
Coffee Cups, 2002

$3\frac{1}{2}$ x 3 x 3 in. each
(8.9 x 7.6 x 7.6 cm)
Wheel-thrown porcelain;
gas fired, cone 10
Photo by artist

RICHARD HENSLEY
Blue Cup, 2003

4½ x 4 in.
(11.4 x 10.2 cm)
Wheel-thrown porce-
lain; reduction fired,
cone 10
Photo by Tim Barnwell

1757 HARRIS DELLER
Untitled, 2004

4½ x 6 x 5 in.
(11.4 x 15.2 x 12.7 cm)
Wheel-thrown and hand-built
porcelain; reduction fired, cone
10; celadon glaze, incised pattern
Photo by artist

IN THIS CUP, THE HANDLE AND
VOLUME ARE DISTINCT ELEMENTS
WORKING TOGETHER TO BECOME
A WHOLE. PATTERN IS USED TO
ACTIVATE AND GIVE CHARACTER
TO THE VOLUME AS THE HANDLE
ENTERS AND EXITS IT.

KATE S. MURRAY
Set of Four Three-Color Mugs, 2001

4 x 3½ x 2½ in. each
(10.2 x 8.9 x 6.4 cm)
Thrown stoneware; reduction,
cone 11; wax resist
Photos by artist

KATHRYNE KOOP
Tan Mug, 2003

5½ x 2¾ x 4¾ in.
(14 x 7 x 12 cm)
Wheel-thrown porcelain; gas
fired in reduction, cone 11;
multiple glazes
Photo by Bruce Spielman

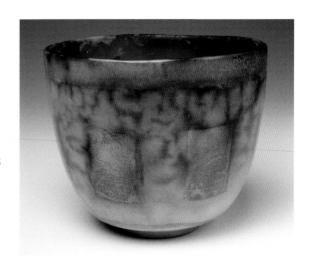

MIGUEL A. ABUGATTAS
Untitled, 2003

4 x 4½ x 4½ in.
(10.2 x 11.4 x 11.4 cm)
Wheel-thrown porcelain;
burnished, bisqued, and
masked; smoke fired
Photo by Lee Schwabe

BETH ROHMAN
The X-Cups, 2003

3¾ x 3 in. each (9.5 x 7.6 cm)
Wheel-thrown and altered porcelain;
gas fired in reduction, cone 10; wax
resist, shino glazes
Photo by Sharon Belttary

DANNON RHUDY | 4 x 4½ x 4½ in.
Porcelain Landscapes VII, 2002 | (10.2 x 11.4 x 11.4 cm)
Thrown and altered porcelain;
wood fired, cones 11–12
Photo by artist

KAREN ANNE BOLTON | 6 x 3 x 3 in.
Wood-Fired Cup, 2004 | (15.2 x 7.6 x 7.6 cm)
Wheel-thrown stoneware; wood
fired in anagama kiln, cone 12
Photo by artist

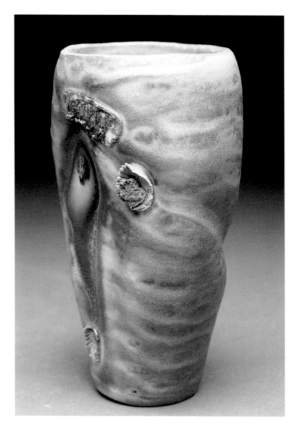

CHUCK McGEE
Coolie, 2003

5 x 3 x 4 in.
(12.7 x 7.6 x 10.2 cm)
Wheel-thrown and altered
porcelain; wood fired, cone 10;
double-walled construction
Photo by artist

JOSEPH BRUHIN
Tea Bowl, 2002

3 x 4 x 4 in.
(7.6 x 10.2 x 10.2 cm)
Porcelain; wood fired
Photo by Michael Crow

BRIAN J. TAYLOR
Bound, 2003

3 x 3 x 3 in.
(7.6 x 7.6 x 7.6 cm)
Wheel-thrown and textured
white stoneware; soda fired,
cone 10
Photo by artist

TODD LEECH
Set of Three Tea Bowls, 2003

4 x 4 x 4 in. each (10.2 x 10.2 x 10.2 cm)
Wheel-thrown stoneware; gas fired in
reduction, cone 10
Photo by Heather Protz

MARTA MATRAY GLOVICZKI
Vodka Cups, 2002

3 x 1½ x 1½ in. each
(7.6 x 3.8 x 3.8 cm)
Hand-built porcelain; gas
fired with soda, cone 10
Photo by Peter Lee

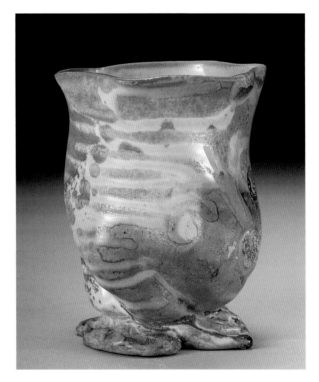

JOY LAPPIN
Wood Floral Cup

5 x 3½ in. (12.7 x 8.9 cm)
Wheel-thrown and altered
stoneware; wood fired in
reduction in anagama
kiln, cones 10–11; natural
fly ash glaze
Photo by Tony Deck

313

STEPHEN GRIMMER
Two Bourbon Cups, 2003

4 x 3 x 3 in. each (10.2 x 7.6 x 7.6 cm)
Wheel-thrown stoneware; reduction
fired, cone 10; slip and glaze
Photo by artist

LINDA MCFARLING
Faceted Yonomi, 2003

4½ x 3½ x 3½ in.
(11.4 x 8.9 x 8.9 cm)
Thrown and faceted
stoneware; salt/soda
fired, cone 10
Photo by Tom Mills

JASON HESS
Faceted Cups, 2004

4½ x 3 x 3 in. each
(11.4 x 7.6 x 7.6 cm)
Stoneware; wood fired with soda
Photo by artist

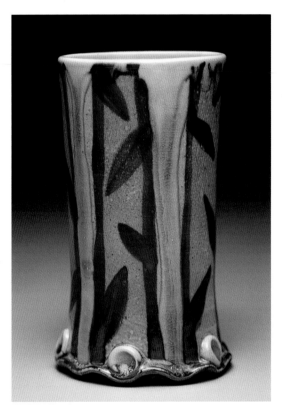

BETHANY BENSON
Cup, 2003

6½ x 3¼ in.
(16.5 x 8.3 cm)
Thrown and altered white
stoneware; soda fired, cone 10;
black slip decoration with glaze
Photo by artist

AMY LENHARTH
Shino Goblet 2004

9 x 4 x 4 in.
(22.9 x 10.2 x 10.2 cm)
Thrown porcelain; gas fired
in reduction, cone 10;
shino with wax resist
Photo by Janet Ryan

JAMES TINGEY | 9 x 9 x 4 in. each (22.9 x 22.9 x 10.2 cm)
Stacked Cups, 2002 | Thrown and slipped porcelain and
stoneware; salt fired in reduction, cone 10
Photo by Joe Davis

BEN KRUPKA
Lineup, 2003

4 x 3½ x 3½ in. each
(10.2 x 8.9 x 8.9 cm)
Wheel-thrown and altered porcelain;
wood fired in reduction, cone 10
Photo by artist

TARA WILSON | 4 x 8 x 4 in. each
Cups, 2003 | (10.2 x 20.3 x 10.2 cm)
| Thrown and altered stoneware;
| wood fired, cone 10
| Photo by artist

LISA BARRY
Cup Form, 2003

5 x 4½ x 3 in.
(12.7 x 11.4 x 7.6 cm)
Thrown porcelain; soda
fired, cone 10
Photo by Matt Mihlik

JOHN ELDER
Mug, 2003

5 x 4¹⁄₂ x 4 in.
(12.7 x 11.4 x 10.2 cm)
Thrown stoneware; single
fired in two-chamber
Noborigama wood kiln,
lightly salted; slip,
brushed glaze
Photo by artist

I LIKE MY WORK TO FEEL
RELAXED, WITH ONE FOOT IN
TRADITION AND THE OTHER IN
THE CONTEMPORARY WORLD.

MEIRA MATHISON
Mug, 2004

4¹⁄₂ x 3 in. (11.4 x 7.6 cm)
Thrown and altered porce-
lain, colored-clay additions;
cone 10; thick slip, multi-
layered glazes
Photo by Janet Dwyer

CATHI JEFFERSON
Latte Cups, 2003

5 x 4 x 4 in. each
(12.7 x 10.2 x 10.2 cm)
Wheel-thrown and altered
stoneware; salt and soda fired
Photo by Hans Sipma

JOHN A. ULERY | 3 x 4 x 4 in.
Cup, 2003 | (7.6 x 10.2 x 10.2 cm)
Wheel-thrown and assembled
white stoneware; salt and
soda fired, cone 10
Photo by Sarah L. Rossiter

PEG MALLOY
Two Mugs with Crackle Slip, 2003

4¾ x 5 x 3½ in. each (12 x 12.7 x 8.9 cm)
Wheel-thrown white stoneware; wood
fired, cone 11; crackle slip applied to
bisque; re-bisqued; black slip
Photo by artist

RACHEL BERG
Moonlit Garden Sake Cup, 2003

2½ x 2 x 2 in. (6.4 x 5 x 5 cm)
Thrown and hand-built
stoneware; soda fired, cone 10;
impressed patterns
Photo by artist

PEGGY STRAIN | 5½ x 3 ½ in. (14 x 8.9 cm)
Leaf Cup, 2004 | Thrown and carved porcelain;
gas fired, cone 10
Photo by Elizabeth Ellingson

JUDITH DUFF | 4 x 6 x 6 in. (10.2 x 15.2 x 15.2 cm)
Cup and Saucer, 2003 | Wheel-thrown and faceted
porcelain; gas fired in reduction,
cone 10; turquoise glaze
Photo by Tom Mills

CHUCK McGEE
Coolie, 2002

5½ x 3 x 4 in.
(14 x 7.6 x 10.2 cm)
Wheel-thrown and altered
porcelain; wood fired in
anagama kiln, cone 10;
shino glaze, double-walled
construction
Photo by artist

JIM CONNELL
Green Carved Cup, 2003

4½ x 4½ x 4½ in.
(11.4 x 11.4 x 11.4 cm)
Thrown and carved porcelain;
salt fired, cone 10
Photo by artist

BRAD SCHWIEGER
Cup Construction, 2004

9 x 10 x 5 in. (22.9 x 25.4 x 12.7 cm)
Wheel-thrown and altered stoneware;
soda fired, cone 10; multiple slips and
glazes, nichrome wire
Photo by artist

MICHAEL T. SCHMIDT
Cup(s) and Saucer(s), 2001

Cups: 4¼ x 1¾ in. each (10.8 x 4.4 cm)
Wheel-thrown stoneware; soda fired,
cone 10; nichrome wire handles
Photo by artist

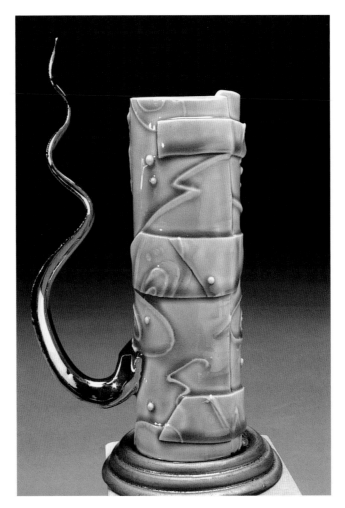

DAVID PENDELL
Cool Jazz Cup, 2002

7½ x 4½ x 3½ in.
(19 x 11.4 x 8.9 cm)
Hand-built earthenware; electric
fired, cone 04; luster, cone 018
Photo by artist

JEREMY HATCH | 6 x 5 x 4 in. (15.2 x 12.7 x 10.2 cm)
Cup, 2001 | Wheel-thrown and assembled
porcelain; electric fired, cone 7;
plastic tubing
Photos by Ying-Yueh Chuang

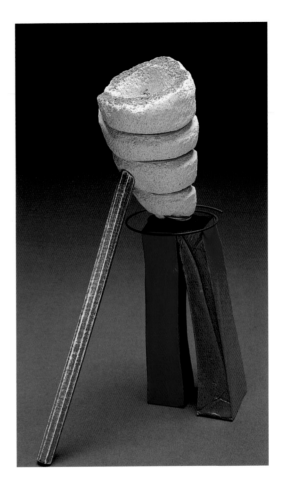

TONY MARTIN | 13¼ x 4 x 6½ in.
Mug II/Cup, 2004 | (33.7 x 10.2 x 16.5 cm)
Hand-built stoneware; electric
fired, cone 06; low-fire glazes
and stains, cone 012
Photo by Julie Hillebrant

KEN HORVATH | 9 x 6 x 3 in.
Cup #3, 1999 | (22.9 x 15.2 x 7.6 cm)
Thrown and slab-built earth-
enware; electric fired, cone
04; acrylic stain, cone 022
Photo by artist
Courtesy of Mudfire Gallery

KEVIN L. TURNER
Solenopsis Cups, 2004

16 x 6 x 4 in. each
(40.6 x 15.2 x 10.2 cm)
Hand-built and slip-cast porcelain;
reduction fired, cone 10; glazed
and sanded surface
Photo by artist

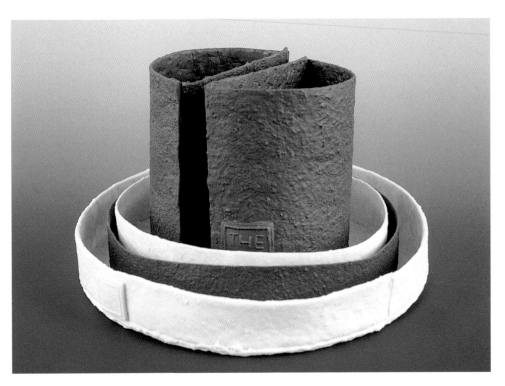

BILLIE JEAN THEIDE
Cups and Trays, 2002

3 x 5 x 5 in. (7.6 x 12.7 x 12.7 cm)
Hand-built Polish porcelain; gas
fired in reduction, 2516°F (1380°C)
Photo by artist

JOHN GOODHEART
Cups For a Sinner, 2001

12 x 10 x 6 in. each
(30.5 x 25.4 x 15.2 cm)
Thrown earthenware; electric fired,
cone 05; fabricated metal parts
Photo by Michael Cavanaugh
and Kevin Montague

JOHN KUDLACEK
Dysfunctional Cup, 2002

6¾ x 4½ x 4½ in.
(17.2 x 11.4 x 11.4 cm)
Thrown and hand-built porcelain;
gas fired in reduction, cone 10;
glazed interior, unglazed exterior
Photo by Michael Regnier

DODIE CAMPBELL
White Egg Cup, 2003

2 x 4 x 2 in. (5 x 10.2 x 5 cm)
Altered and assembled slip-cast
porcelain; gas fired, cone 10
Photo by Nathan Campbell and artist

SUSAN FILLEY | 4 x 3½ x 3½ in.
Snowflake Red Cup, 2004 | (10.2 x 8.9 x 8.9 cm)
| Thrown porcelain;
| reduction, cone 10; triple-
| dipped crystal red glaze
| Photo by artist

DIMITAR PETROV PETROV | 6 x 2¼ x 2¼ in.
Series Cup: | (15.2 x 5.7 x 5.7 cm)
The New World I, 2003 | Gypsum-cast porcelain;
| electric fired, 2156°F
| (1180°C); decals,
| 1427°F (775°C)
| Photo by Vasil Germanov

REENA KASHYAP
Pair of Drips, 2004

3¾ x 9½ x 2¾ in. each (9.5 x 24.1 x 7 cm)
Wheel-thrown and altered porcelain;
gas fired in reduction, cone 10;
trailed white satin matte and
Byron's Oxblood glazes
Photo by artist

LOIS HARBAUGH
Pair: Left and Right, 2004

$3\frac{1}{2}$ x $5\frac{1}{2}$ x 4 in. each
(8.9 x 14 x 10.2 cm)
Wheel-thrown porcelain; gas fired,
cone 10; second firing electric,
cone 05; underglaze line
Photo by Roger Schreiber

EACH CUP HAS A SCALLOPED EDGE FOR
DECORATION AND A STRAIGHT EDGE
FOR DRINKING. WHEN A HANDLE IS
ADDED, THE CUP BECOMES EITHER A
LEFT-HANDED OR RIGHT-HANDED CUP.

DAN ANDERSON
How to Surface Dive, 2003

5 x 5 x 3¾ in.
(12.7 x 12.7 x 9.5 cm)
Wheel-thrown porcelain; soda
fired, cone 10; silk-screened
photo decal, cone 017
Photo by Jeffrey Bruce

KRISTEN KIEFFER
Cups and Saucers, 2004

FORM, FUNCTION, AND ORNAMENTATION ARE OF EQUAL IMPORTANCE TO ME AS A POTTER. MY HOPE IS THAT THE FORMS INVITE CLOSER INSPECTION, WHEN THEY MAY REVEAL THEIR SURFACES, WHICH IN TURN ENTICE THE VIEWER TO HOLD AND USE THEM.

$4\frac{1}{2}$ x $6\frac{1}{2}$ in. each (11.4 x 16.5 cm)
Wheel-thrown and altered white stoneware; soda fired, cone 10; slip trailed
Photo by the artist

REBECCA HARVEY
Cup and Saucer, 2003

3¼ x 5½ x 5½ in.
(8.3 x 14 x 14 cm)
Wheel-thrown and turned
stoneware; soda fired in
reduction, 2372°F (1300°C);
sprayed cobalt slip
Photo by Adrian Newman

S.K. GUSSTIFF
Cup and Saucer, 2003

5 x 5 x 5 in.
(12.7 x 12.7 x 12.7 cm)
Porcelain; oxidation, cone 6;
slips and ash glaze
Photo by Stephen Robison

EMILY REASON
Studded Cup and Saucer, 2003

6 x 7 x 7 in. (15.2 x 17.8 x 17.8 cm)
Thrown, altered, and carved porcelain;
salt and soda fired, cone 10
Photo by artist

S.K. GUSSTIFF
Cup and Saucer, 2003

5 x 5 x 5 in. (12.7 x 12.7 x 12.7 cm)
Porcelain; oxidation, cone 6; slips
and ash glaze
Photo by Stephen Robison

A MAJOR OBJECTIVE FOR ME IS TO CREATE
TACTILE QUALITIES IN OBJECTS OF USE AND
DOMESTICITY, OFFERING AN INTIMATE
RELATIONSHIP WITH THE USER AND GIVING
THE OBJECTS LIVES OF THEIR OWN.

DEBORAH SCHWARTZKOPF
Two Cups and Saucers, 2001

Cups: 5 x 6 in. each (12.7 x 15.2 cm)
Hand-built porcelain; salt fired in
reduction, cone 10
Photo by artist

JUDY THOMPSON
Cup and Saucer, 2003

3½ x 4¼ x 2¼ in.
(8.9 x 10.8 x 5.7 cm)
Wheel-thrown porcelain;
oxidation fired, cone 6
Photo by artist

THE QUEST TO PRODUCE THE
PERFECT MUG HAS TAKEN
YEARS...STILL NOT THERE...BUT
GETTING CLOSER. MAYBE IT'S
ABOUT THE JOURNEY.

CONNER BURNS
Cup and Saucer, 2001

3 x 5 x 4½ in.
(7.6 x 12.7 x 11.4 cm)
Wheel-thrown and
altered white stoneware;
gas fired in reduction,
cone 10; ash glaze
Photo by Al Surratt

MICHAEL CONNELLY
Handled Cups, 2004

Left: 6 x 3 x 3 in. (15.2 x 7.6 x 7.6 cm)
Right: 5 x 3 x 3 in. (12.7 x 7.6 x 7.6 cm)
Wheel-thrown white stoneware;
soda fired, cone 10
Photo by artist

EMILY MURPHY
Striped Mugs, 2003

4½ x 4¼ x 3 in. each (11.4 x 10.8 x 7.6 cm)
Wheel-thrown stoneware; soda fired in
reduction, cone 10; flashing slips
Photo by Guy Nicol

BETH ROHMAN
Sake Cup, 2003

$3\frac{1}{2}$ x 3 in. (8.9 x 7.6 cm)
Wheel-thrown porcelain; gas
fired in reduction, cone 10;
wax resist, shino glazes
Photo by Sharon Belttary

TONY MOORE
Wood-Fired Shino Cup, 2003

3 x 4½ x 4½ in. (7.6 x 11.4 x 11.4 cm)
Wheel-thrown and incised stoneware;
wood fired with light salt, cone 10;
shino glaze, willow ash decoration
Photo by Howard Goodman

SCOTT A. BENNETT
Gutter Cup, 2002

5½ x 5 x 3 in.
(14 x 12.7 x 7.6 cm)
Extruded and press-molded terra
cotta; electric fired, cone 04; glazed
Photo by artist

ANDERSON MORRIS BAILEY
Daintyfoot Mug with Magic Shapes, 2004

5½ x 3½ x 3½ in.
(14 x 8.9 x 8.9 cm)
Wheel-thrown porcelain;
soda fired, cone 10
Photo by John Lucas

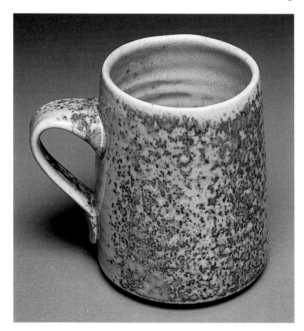

CRYSTAL RIBICH
Wood-Fired Cup, 2003

4 x 4¼ x 3 in.
(10.2 x 10.8 x 7.6 cm)
Wheel-thrown porcelain; wood
fired, cone 10; shino slip
Photo by Tony Rinaldo

RYAN J. GREENHECK
Handled Cup, 2003

I ENJOY THE FACT THAT SOME-
ONE WILL PICK UP ONE OF MY
CUPS BY THE HANDLE AND FEEL
COMPELLED TO EXPLORE THE
FORM WITH THE OPPOSITE HAND.

4½ x 4 x 3½ in.
(11.4 x 10.2 x 8.9 cm)
Porcelain; wood fired
Photo by artist

MARIAN BAKER
Green Cup, 2003

4¼ x 4 x 2¾ in.
(10.8 x 10.2 x 7 cm)
Thrown porcelain; electric fired,
cone 6; glaze, wax resist
Photo by Robert Diamante

DALE HUFFMAN | $2\frac{1}{4}$ x $2\frac{3}{4}$ in. (5.7 x 7 cm)
Sake Cup, 2003 | Wheel-thrown stoneware with
silica inclusions; wood fired,
cone 12; natural ash glaze
Photo by artist

JOSH DeWEESE | 5 x 5 x 4 in.
Mugs, 2002 | (12.7 x 12.7 x 10.2 cm)
Wheel-thrown stoneware;
wood fired, cone 11;
fired on shells
Photo by artist

LINDA McFARLING
Yonomi, 2003

4 x 3½ x 3½ in.
(10.2 x 8.9 x 8.9 cm)
Thrown stoneware;
salt/soda fired, cone
10; white slip
Photo by Tom Mills

BONITA COHN
Craquelure, 2002

3⅝ x 4½ x 3¼ in.
(9.2 x 11.4 x 8.3 cm)
Wheel-thrown stoneware; wood
and salt kiln, cone 12; double
bisqued and stained, shino slip
Photo by artist

JOSEPH E. PINTZ
Tea Bowl, 2003

$3\frac{1}{2}$ x $4\frac{1}{2}$ x $4\frac{1}{2}$ in.
(8.9 x 11.4 x 11.4 cm)
Thrown and altered
stoneware; wood fired in
anagama kiln, cone 11;
natural ash glaze
Photo by Jeff Bruce

SHARON D. MORRIS
Two Shino Cups, 2003

Left: $3\frac{1}{2}$ x 4 x $3\frac{1}{8}$ in. (8.9 x 10.2 x 7.9 cm)
Right: $3\frac{3}{4}$ x $4\frac{1}{4}$ x $3\frac{1}{2}$ in. (9.5 x 10.8 x 8.9 cm)
Wheel-thrown brown stoneware; bisque, cone
06; glaze, cones 10–11; apricot shino glaze,
India ink rubbed into crazed areas
Photo by Ken Sanville

JINNY WHITEHEAD
Cup, 2003

2½ x 4 in. (6.4 x 10.2 cm)
Pinched porcelain; wood fired,
cone 12; thin shino glaze
Photo by Eye Q Studios
(Duff & Gravelsins)

GILL MALLINCKRODT
Yonomi #1, 2003

3⅞ x 3⅞ x 3⅞ in.
(9.8 x 9.8 x 9.8 cm)
Wheel-thrown local clay;
fired in anagama kiln,
cone 10; dry shino glaze
Photo by David Egan

JEANNINE MARCHAND
Pinched Cups, 2002

Left: 3 x 3½ in. (7.6 x 8.9 cm)
Right: 4 x 3½ in. (10.2 x 8.9 cm)
Pinched stoneware; gas fired in reduction,
cone 10; copper/manganese wash,
porcelain slip, Tom's Clear glaze
Photo by Tom Mills

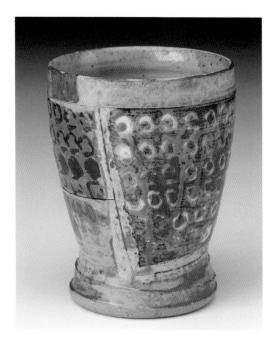

ELIZABETH FLANNERY
Shibori Cup, 2003

3½ x 3 x 3½ in.
(8.9 x 7.6 x 8.9 cm)
Wheel-thrown stoneware;
gas fired in reduction, cone
10; inlaid and layered slips,
brushed glaze
Photo by John Polak

LAUREN GALLASPY
Slitten, 2004

5½ x 3 x 3 in.
(14 x 7.6 x 7.6 cm)
Slab-built porcelain;
electric fired, cone 6
Photo by Walker Montgomery

MAGGIE MAE BEYELER
Tea with Dante, 2003

12 x 5 x 4 in. (30.5 x 12.7 x 10.2 cm)
Hand-built stoneware; electric fired,
cone 6; underglaze text and image
Photo by Chas McGrath

MARY E. BRIGGS | $3\frac{1}{2}$ x $4\frac{3}{4}$ in. (8.9 x 12 cm)
Bird with Blueberries, 2003 | Wheel-thrown terra cotta;
electric fired, cone 04
Photo by Joe Davis

AMANDA LYNCH | 8 x 5 in. (20.3 x 12.7 cm)
Untitled, 2003 | Porcelain; soda fired;
underglaze painting
Photo by Ryan Fowler

KELLY O'BRIANT
Mug with Peas, 2003

$4^{1}/_{2}$ x $3^{1}/_{2}$ x $3^{1}/_{2}$ in.
(11.4 x 8.9 x 8.9 cm)
Wheel-thrown porcelain;
methane gas fired in
reduction, cone $10^{1}/_{2}$;
terra sigillata, oxides,
and celadon glaze
Photo by Tom Mills

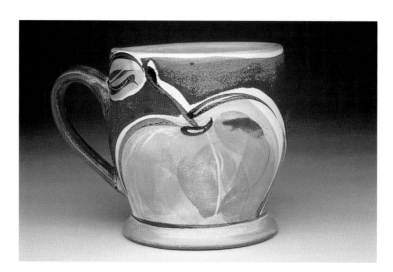

WYNNE WILBUR
Fruit Cup, 2001

4 x 5 x 4 in. (10.2 x 12.7 x 10.2 cm)
Wheel-thrown terra cotta; electric
fired, cone 03; majolica
Photo by artist

ANN TUBBS
Face Mug, 2004

$4\frac{1}{2}$ x $4\frac{1}{2}$ in. (11.4 x 11.4 cm)
Thrown and altered clay;
cone 2; majolica
Photo by Jerry Anthony

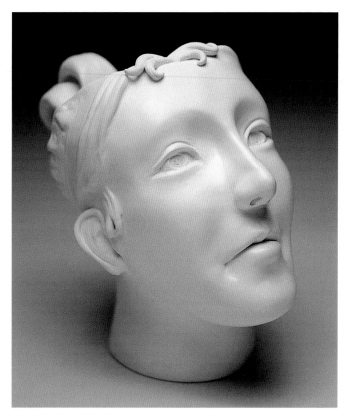

NOBUHITO NISHIGAWARA

Cup, 2003

7 x 5 x 5 in.
(17.8 x 12.7 x 12.7 cm)
Hand-built porcelain; electric
fired, cone 6; polished
Photo by artist

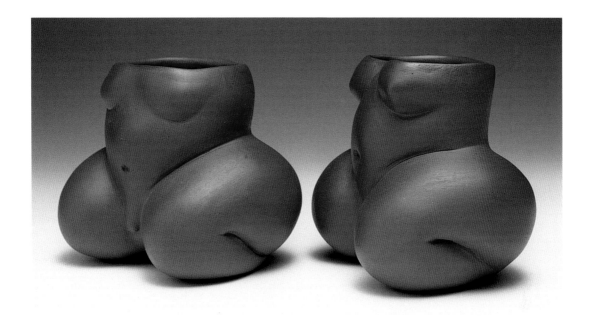

RICHARD SWANSON
He/She, 2003

3 x 3 x 2¾ in. (7.6 x 7.6 x 7 cm)
Fine-grained and high-iron clay; electric
fired, cone 5; cast and sanded after
each firing; fired until vitreous
Photo by artist

THESE CUPS ARE PART OF A SERIES OF VESSELS THAT
ARE INFORMED BY HISTORICAL EXAMPLES—INUIT
CARVINGS, PRE-COLUMBIAN CERAMICS, AFRICAN SCULP-
TURE, JAPANESE NETSUKE CARVINGS, AND YIXING
TEAPOTS. I ADMIRE THE CONCISE VOCABULARY OF
THESE PIECES, THEIR COMPACT FORMAT, AND THEIR
UNIQUE WAY OF RELATING FIGURATIVE ELEMENTS.

JEREMY RANDALL | 6 x 5 x 5 in.
Drift Boat, 2004 | (15.2 x 12.7 x 12.7 cm)
Hand-built porcelain; gas
fired in oxidation, cone 10;
terra sigillatas, washes, glaze
Photo by artist

PAMELA SEGERS
Haunted Forest, 2003

THIS PIECE, FROM A SERIES CALLED
"BENEATH THE PINE TREES," WAS
INSPIRED BY MY EXPERIENCES WORKING
AT A CAMP DURING MY TEENS.

12 x 14 x 8½ in.
(30.5 x 35.6 x 21.6 cm)
Thrown and slab-built; multiple firings,
cone 04; airbrushed velvet underglaze,
silk-screened color decals
Photo by artist

JOHN CHWEKUN
Cup, 2001

5 x 4 x 3 in.
(12.7 x 10.2 x 7.6 cm)
Hollow-constructed
stoneware; electric
fired, cones 6 and 06
Photo by artist

CATHERINE THORNTON
Stump Water, 2004

5 x 4 x 4 in.
(12.7 x 10.2 x 10.2 cm)
Hand- and slab-built porcelain;
electric fired, cone 6; multiple glazes
Photo by Lynn Ruck

I HAVE HEARD COFFEE CALLED "STUMP
WATER" AND SOME BREWS REALLY
DESERVE THAT NAME. I MADE A CUP
FOR TRUE STUMP WATER, INCLUDING A
HEALTHY GROWTH OF LICHEN AND A
FROG IN THE BOTTOM OF THE CUP.

SUSAN BOSTWICK
A Slice of Life #2, 2001

5½ x 6 x 6 in. (14 x 15.2 x 15.2 cm)
Press-molded, thrown, and cast
earthenware; electric fired, cone 04;
multiple fired slips, stains, and glazes
Photo by Joseph Gruber

KURT BRIAN WEBB
Mute Swan: Invasive Species Series, 2004

5½ x 6 x 6 in. (14 x 15.2 x 15.2 cm)
Pinched stoneware; soda fired
Photo by artist

SUSAN M. MACD. COOK
Turtles and Mermaids: Praying for Rain Series, 2004

3 x 3 in. (7.6 x 7.6 cm)
Pinched and carved porcelain; wood fired in anagama kiln, cone 10; glazed interior only
Photo by Margot Geist

CHRIS GUSTIN
Set of Tumblers, 2002

6 x 3 x 3 in. each (15.2 x 7.6 x 7.6 cm)
Wheel-thrown porcelain; wood/soda
fired, cone 11
Photo by Dean Powell

SANDRA TORRES
Green Cups, 2003

USING WATERCOLOR IN PORCELAIN
(SULFATES) ALLOWS ME TO MAINTAIN
THE RAW TEXTURE OF CLAY AND ADD
VERY DIFFERENT COLORS.

Largest: 4 x 3¼ in. (10.2 x 8.3 cm)
Thrown and altered porcelain; gas fired
in reduction, cone 10; bisqueware
dipped in potassium dichromate, clear
glaze interior, unglazed exterior
Photo by artist

SUSAN BEINER | 5 x 4½ x 3 in. each
Butt Cups, 2003 | (12.7 x 11.4 x 7.6 cm)
| Slip-cast porcelain; gas fired, cone 6
| Photo by Susan Einstein

MILA VISSER 'T HOOFT | 3 x 3 x 3 in.
Yonomi, 2003 | (7.6 x 7.6 x 7.6 cm)
| Wheel-thrown
| porcelain; wood fired,
| cone 11; ash glaze
| Photo by Richard Sargent

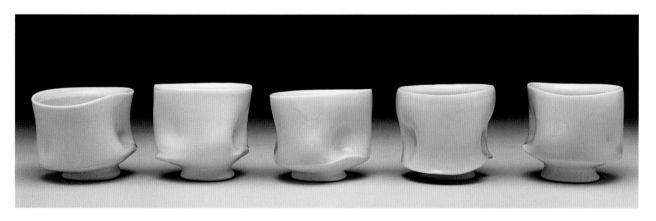

DAVID PIPER | $2\frac{1}{2}$ x 10 x 2 in. each (6.4 x 25.4 x 5 cm)
Five Sake Cups, 2003 | Thrown porcelain; reduction fired,
| cone 9; celadon glazes
| Photo by Leslie Bauer

LORNA MEADEN | 4 x 4 x 3 in. (10.2 x 10.2 x 7.6 cm)
Untitled, 2003 | Thrown and altered porcelain;
oxidation fired, cone 10
Photo by artist

RICHARD HENSLEY | 4½ x 4 in. each (11.4 x 10.2 cm)
Three Cups, 2003 | Wheel-thrown porcelain; reduction
fired, cone 10
Photo by Tim Barnwell

LUCY FAGELLA
Green Goblet, 2003

THIS GREEN GOBLET HINTS AT THE TALL,
GREEN GRASSES FROM MY FARMING DAYS.

5 x 3 in. (12.7 x 7.6 cm)
Thrown and altered porcelain;
electric fired, cone 6
Photo by John Polak

KATHRYN E. NARROW
Peach Cup, 2003

3½ x 4¼ x 4¼ in.
(8.9 x 10.8 x 10.8 cm)
Thrown, carved, and
repoussé porcelain;
electric fired, cone 6
Photo by John Carlano

BARBARA HOFFMAN
Celadon Teacup, 2003

3 x 3 x 3 in. (7.6 x 7.6 x 7.6 cm)
Wheel-thrown porcelain; gas fired in
reduction, cone 10; carved
Photo by John Bonath

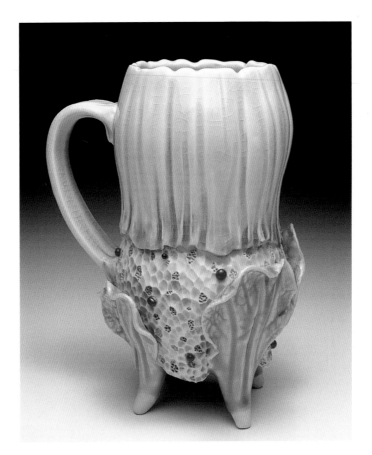

BONNIE SEEMAN | 6 x 4 x 4 in. (15.2 x 10.2 x 10.2 cm)
Untitled, 2004 | Wheel-thrown and altered porcelain;
electric fired, cone 10
Photo by artist

JOANNA STECKER
Teacup and Pillow, 2003

6 x 5 x 4½ in.
(15.2 x 12.7 x 11.4 cm)
Thrown and hand-built porcelain;
electric fired, cone 6
Photo by Bart Kaston

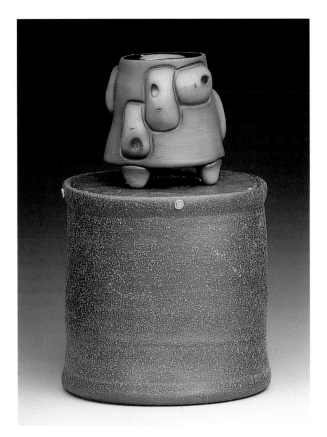

KATHLEEN GUSS
STEPHEN ROBISON
Scotch Cup and Box, 2003

Cup: 3 x 2 x 2 in.
(7.6 x 5 x 5 cm)
Box: 5 x 5 x 5 in.
(12.7 x 12.7 x 12.7 cm)
Thrown and hand-built
stoneware; reduction fired,
cone 10; terra sigillata
Photo by Stephen Robison

JOHN GOODHEART
A Cup For Judgment Day, 2001

14 x 7 x 6 in.
(35.6 x 17.8 x 15.2 cm)
Thrown earthenware; electric fired,
cone 05; fabricated metal parts
Photo by Michael Cavanaugh
and Kevin Montague

BRADLEY KEYS | 9 x 12 x 5 in. (22.9 x 30.5 x 12.7 cm)
Tea For Two, 2004 | Thrown and altered red stoneware;
electric fired, cone 6; slips with
sprayed glaze; oak stand
Photo by artist

HEATHER O'BRIEN
Dessert Cups on Stand, 2002

I DESIGN PIECES SPECIFICALLY AROUND RITUALS.
THE INTENDED USE IS NOT READILY APPARENT,
BUT VIEWERS GET THE SENSE THAT THE PIECES
ARE MEANT TO BE USED AT LEAST FOR SPECIAL
OCCASIONS. I AM INSPIRED BY THE CUSTOMS
THAT SURROUND THE MANNERS AND OCCASIONS
OF DINING, BOTH FROM MY OWN LIFE AND FROM
OTHER CULTURES.

16 in. length (40.6 cm)
Slab- and coil-built porcelain and black
clay; electric fired, cone 6
Photo by Luis Garcia

SHEILA CLENNELL | 6 x 12 x 3 in. (15.2 x 30.5 x 7.6 cm)
Sake Cups, 2003 | Thrown stoneware; reduction fired
on a firebrick table, cone 10; carbon
trap shino
Photo by Tony Clennell

TARA WILSON
Cup and Saucer, 2003

5 x 5 x 5 in. (12.7 x 12.7 x 12.7 cm)
Thrown and altered stoneware;
wood fired, cone 10
Photo by artist

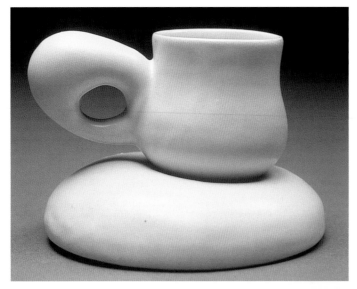

HANNAH FISHER
White Cup with Pillow, 2003

3½ x 4 x 3 in.
(8.9 x 10.2 x 7.6 cm)
Thrown porcelain;
soda fired, cone 10
Photo by artist

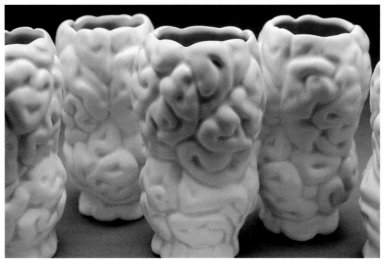

MEREDITH HOST
Brain Tumblers, 2004

6 x 3 x 3 in. (15.2 x 7.6 x 7.6 cm)
Slip-cast porcelain; electric fired,
cone 6
Photo by artist

JUAN GRANADOS
Four Tumblers, 2004

4¼ x 3¼ x 3¼ in. each
(10.8 x 8.3 x 8.3 cm)
Wheel-thrown and hand-altered
white stoneware; glaze, cone 10
Photo by artist

KAREN SWYLER
Conjoin, 2003

6 x 11 x 6 in. (15.2 x 27.9 x 15.2 cm)
Wheel-thrown and altered porcelain;
electric fired, cone 10
Photo by artist

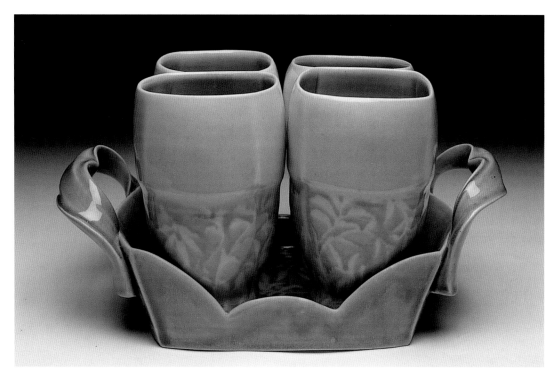

BRENDA QUINN
Juice Cups with Tray, 2003

6 x 7 1/2 x 6 in. (15.2 x 19 x 15.2 cm)
Thrown and altered porcelain; gas fired
in oxidation, cone 10
Photo by artist

BARBARA KNUTSON
Spirals and Fish Cup, 2001

$4\frac{1}{2}$ x 6 x $3\frac{1}{2}$ in.
(11.4 x 15.2 x 8.9 cm)
Slab-built and wheel-
thrown white stoneware;
reduction fired, cone 10
Photo by Randy Battista

JOANNE TAYLOR BROWN
Ocean Cup, 2002

5 x 5 x 4 in. (12.7 x 12.7 x 10.2 cm)
Slab-built porcelain; reduction fired,
cone 10; celadon glaze
Photo by John Carlano

CHRIS CUNNINGHAM | 5 x 3 x 5 in. (12.7 x 7.6 x 12.7 cm)
Snail Cup, 2003 | Wheel-thrown and altered
stoneware; gas fired, cone 10;
electric fired, cone 06
Photo by artist

JANE MURPHY
Cup, 2004

4 x 3¼ x 3½ in.
(10.2 x 8.3 x 8.9 cm)
Wheel-thrown and altered
stoneware; raku reduction;
bisque, cone 04
Photo by Joseph McDonald

1866 LAUREN HERZAK-BAUMAN
Black-and-White Cups, 2003

7 x 3 x 3¼ in. each
(17.8 x 7.6 x 8.3 cm)
Thrown porcelain; fired in
downdraft gas, cone 10
Photo by artist

MYRA KAHA
Cup, 2004

6¼ x 3 x 3 in.
(15.9 x 7.6 x 7.6 cm)
Porcelain; soda fired, cone 10
Photo by artist

Acknowledgments

Over 1,000 ceramic artists submitted images of their very best cups for this book, and we owe them our sincere appreciation for allowing us to consider their work for it, and for their continued interest in our showcase series. Thanks also to jurors Tom and Elaine Coleman, who spent many hours in attentive contemplation of the thousands of entries, bringing their many years' experience in clay art to the task. Behind the scenes, many helpful Lark staffers provided huge amounts of support, good humor, and just plain hard work: Rebecca Guthrie, Rosemary Kast, Jeff Hamilton, and Delores Gosnell, as well as editorial interns Meghan McGuire and Amanda Wheeler. Finally, I'm grateful to Barbara Zaretsky, Shannon Yokeley, and Kathy Holmes, whose design sensibilities gave such grace to this volume.

—Suzanne J.E. Tourtillott,
Editor

Contributing Artists